I Curse You with joy

ALSO BY TIFFANY HADDISH

The Last Black Unicorn

Layla, the Last Black Unicorn

I Curse You with joy

TIFFANY HADDISH

DIVERSION
BOOKS

NEW YORK

Diversion Books
A division of Diversion Publishing Corp.
www.diversionbooks.com

Diversion Books and colophon are registered trademarks
of Diversion Publishing Corp.

For more information, email info@diversionbooks.com

First Diversion Books Edition: May 2024
Hardcover ISBN 978-1-635-76953-1
e-ISBN 978-1-635-76945-6

Book design by Neuwirth & Associates, Inc.

Printed in the United States of America
10   9   8   7   6   5   4   3   2   1

Diversion books are available at special discounts for bulk purchases
in the US by corporations, institutions, and other organizations.
For more information, please contact admin@diversionbooks.com.

CONTENTS

Author's Note vii

Introduction ix

A Little Something You Need to Know xv

Brave New World 1

Sex Ed 15

If You Want to Get With Me 27

Daddy Issues 37

My Inheritance—
   A Big Ass and an F'ed-Up View of Relationships 57

Can I Get a Witness? 73

Shark Week 87

Big Tiff Energy 99

Live from New York 109

Elelele 123

Hey Ladies 135

How I Keep My Ass in Check 147

O, Nicolas Cage 153

Body Yaddi Yaddi 159

I See You, South Central 167

Tea with an OG 179

You Get What You Give 195

Blessings 207

Honeypot 221

I Curse You with Joy 231

About the Author 233

AUTHOR'S NOTE

Every story in this book is exactly how I remember what happened. Now, how I remember it might not be how everyone else involved remembers it because, like in my TV show *The Afterparty*, everyone has their own version of events. This one is mine.

INTRODUCTION

PEOPLE TELL ME I'M a celebrity, but I don't always feel like one. If I'm a celebrity, where was my celebration? Did I miss it? Did y'all have a party without me? For the most part, I feel like I'm a regular person. I buy my own maxi pads. I walk my dog and pick up her poo in a plastic bag. And I do my own laundry because I don't need anyone sniffing my panties. But there was one thing that happened that made me think I must be pretty famous after all, and that was when Madame Tussauds wax museum asked if they could do a statue of me.

Let me tell you, it is a *process* to get a wax figure made of your body. They don't just push the model of you out of a mold, pop a wig on top, and you good. It takes almost as long as it does to make a real human, but with less fucking at the beginning. I had to go to this office building in LA to pose for the staff while they measured my eyebrows, my chin, my forehead, my eyes, my elbows, my belly, and my feet. They got my corns, bunions, everything. They got so intimate with my nooks and crannies, I thought they were going to take me out to breakfast the next day.

A few months later, when it was time for me to see the result, I showed up for the unveiling a little early so I could sneak a peek one-on-one. I made my way past Michael Jackson, Stevie Wonder, Drake, Rihanna, Gwen Stefani, and Big Poppa. Nicki Minaj was in there, too. Muhammad Ali, Shaq. Like the best party you've never been to.

When I got past Biggie Smalls, I stopped. There she was. There *I* was. Damn, she looked just like me.

Girlfriend looked *good*. They'd put her in my white Alexander McQueen dress that I'd worn to the *Girls Trip* premiere (and then again to the Academy Awards, and to the MTV Movie Awards, and to like six other places because that gown was *expensive*). She had one hand on her hip and she was serving with the other. The nose was right. The mouth was right. The legs, the arms, the hairline—it was all on point. They had used real human hair for everything—on the scalp, eyelashes, eyebrows. I didn't check what was under the hood, so I dunno what they did for the lady bits. Probably had some curly hairs in their tool kits. Even the creases in the hand matched the ones in my hand. I thought, *I don't need to have children now. If I had a baby with myself, this is what it would look like.* The sculptors had done an incredible job.

And yet . . .

I don't even know how to describe what was bothering me. Even though that statue was perfect—and I mean *perfect*—it wasn't. It was partly me, but not all the way me. I stared at her a minute before I realized what was giving me the heebie-jeebies.

That statue didn't have any hurt in her eyes. Well, yeah, I know she's a mannequin, so I guess that made sense, but her life looked like it had been real good. She was just standing there, being pretty, enjoying her success. What made her look different from me is that I've had my share of pain in my life. Maybe more than my share.

I have always wanted to be a person who brought joy and laughter to other people because I know what it feels like to be sad. I know what it feels like to hurt and what it feels like to see other people hurt. One of the worst things in life is when you feel like you're the only one who is hurting 'cause it feels like God has it out for you. But y'all, it doesn't matter what kind of shit you're going through; you are not the only one hurting. That's why I've decided to share some of mine in this book—not because I want to bring you down, but because I want you to know you aren't the only one out here fucking up and feeling bad.

I used to hide a lot of the hard parts about my life because I didn't want people to feel sorry for me or give me any pity. But then, as I got more successful, people started asking me, "How did you do it, Tiffany? How is your life so great?" I realized if I hide the mistakes I've made, I'm going to give people the wrong idea. There's going to be some little girl out there thinking that if she messes up, that's it. Game over. No chance of having a good life.

So now when I fuck up, I *Eight Mile* that shit, naming my weaknesses before anyone else can. I'll say, "Look, y'all. I had two hours of sleep yesterday, I was constipated with a doo-doo baby, and I fucked up a lot of lines in rehearsal. I'm going to do better today." If I tell everyone where I messed up, can't nobody make me feel shame for it. If I just say my truth, there's no weapon you can hold against me, unless it's a spear or something.

Okay, for example, let me tell you real quick about my bad day at work.

I was out in Miami to do a New Year's Eve show. I don't know if you've ever been in Miami, but that's where the devil lives. You gotta be careful. I didn't know, but I found out.

The night before the show, I made a bad decision. Instead of getting a good night's sleep like I should have, I went out with all my friends who had come to town to see my show. I partied my ass off, dancing, laughing, and drinking more than I ever drank in my whole entire life. I drank a bunch of drinks that looked like water and tasted like fire. I partied all night, then I partied all morning. Man, I was so messed up, I'm pretty sure I peed in the Uber. My rating definitely went down.

By the time I got dropped off at the venue for the show, my eyes would not open. I stank like a slab of meat that had been marinating in alcohol and I was hurting so bad I thought my kidneys were gonna fall out of my body. I made my way backstage where I passed out and let them put my makeup on like I was a corpse getting ready for an open casket. She was not ready. But four thousand people had paid to see me perform, so I walked out onstage like there wasn't shit wrong with me.

You might have heard what happened next. Let's just say that show was not up to the normal Tiffany Haddish status. It was horrible. I BOMBED. Not a cute bomb like a missile test out in the desert where you scare the shit out of some lizards. Like a big fucking killed-all-the-dogs-and-goats-in-the-village bomb. Guts everywhere. It was not pretty. Lesson learned. Do not get blackout drunk the night before a big day.

I wanted to talk about that disastrous night in my special *Black Mitzvah*, but everyone told me not to. When I say "everyone," I mean two people in particular, but I'm not naming names because I want everyone on my team to know they are important to me and I will protect them. They said, "That's not funny, Tiffany. No one is going to laugh with you. They're going to be laughing *at you*, like you're a fool." I thought, *Well, as long as they're laughing . . . Nobody's perfect every day at work. We all have sins. We are all imperfect creatures.* When I meet somebody who appears to be perfect, I think they must be an alien or they're hiding kids in the basement or something. Every time I make a mistake, I learn from it. That's how I grow. Maybe if I talked about the lessons I've learned, the people who heard me could grow, too.

So, I told the story of my Miami show onstage during my special, and you know what? People fucking *loved* it. You should have heard the audience hoot and holler. They laughed so hard I could feel it in my chest.

When I perform, I trust my audience is there for the laughs, but I think they are also there for a connection to something real. So, reader, that's what I'm offering you here: something real. I'm going to start off with a couple of funny pieces to get you warmed up, but it's not just a yuckity-yuck book. I'm going to get into some deep shit, too, because I'm a storyteller. I'm going to tell you some stories about times I ate it, mistakes I've made, hard things I've been through, and how all of that made me stronger than I ever thought I could be. My hope is that if you listen to my stories about my mistakes, maybe you won't make those same mistakes or maybe you won't feel like you're the only one in the world who screws up. You see my wins, maybe that will help you achieve those same wins. Or you see me do something good, and you figure out how you can do it even better than I did. Sometimes I'm good, sometimes I suck, but I don't want to live my life as a professional victim. I'd rather be a professional overcomer.

Now you might be wondering why there are a few events that I don't discuss in this book. I can hear you saying, "Bitch, do you think we forgot? Why you didn't say anything about that?" There are certain things that I didn't include in this book because they've been put to rest, and I'm not in the business of digging up the dead.

But the rest of the time, the wig is off. I'm not wearing any makeup. No nails. No lashes. I'm going to spill the tea on my life, all the stuff that makes me more alive, more human, and way more interesting than that beautiful, beautiful wax mannequin. Parts of this book are going to be funny—if you're reading it in public and trying not to laugh, people might think there's something wrong with you—but I hope the jokes have more meaning once you see how everything I've been through shaped who I am.

You ready?

A LITTLE SOMETHING
YOU NEED TO KNOW

BEFORE WE GET STARTED, did y'all know I wrote a whole other book? Well, I did. It's called *The Last Black Unicorn* [pause for dramatic effect], and it was a mother-effing *New York Times* bestseller. In that book, I wrote about the best sex of my life, why I call myself a unicorn, how my thrifty ass used a Groupon for a swamp tour I went on with Will Smith and Jada Pinkett Smith—two people who definitely do not need to worry about saving $37.50—and the time I accidentally killed a man at a bar mitzvah with my booty (don't sweat; he was really old, and he died happy). I also included a whole lot about my upbringing, which had its ups and downs.

If You Read *The Last Black Unicorn* . . .

Thank you! I hope you enjoyed it. I put a lot of work into that book, and it makes me happy when I hear people found something in it that made them smile. I have noticed people who read my first book have a lot of the same questions for me after they're done, so I'm going to

xvi   A LITTLE SOMETHING YOU NEED TO KNOW

answer them for you here. If you didn't read *The Last Black Unicorn*, jump to the next section so you can catch up on what you need to know before you dig into this book.

When Was the Last Time You Shit in Someone's Shoes?

I am in my forties now—a full-grown adult woman—so it's been a minute since I personally doo-doo'd in anyone's Jordans. However, after I told my sister the story I shared in *The Last Black Unicorn* about how I shit in my boyfriend's shoes when he stepped out on me, she told her white girlfriend who lived in Tallahassee. A few weeks later, this girl found out *her* boyfriend was cheating on her. Soon as she heard, she knew just what she was going to do. He had just got a new car, so she went off and doo-doo'd and put it in a plastic bag. She got into his car, opened up the glove compartment, and plopped it all over. Now, Tallahassee is in *Florida*—that's a swamp—so you know that was some liquid doo-doo sliding around on his owner's manual.

She heard from his friends that he drove that car for weeks, wondering where the shit smell was coming from, but he couldn't find it. Then one night, he got pulled over by the police. When he went to pull out his registration, there was doodie all over it. Payback's a bitch, cheater. I'm so happy I was able to inspire that even if I didn't have a hand in it myself.

Now that I'm older and further along in my career, I've got better methods of revenge.

There were so many dudes who hated on me as I was coming up, saying things like, "Tiffany, you ain't shit. I don't know why you wasting your time with these acting classes. You're not going to be anything. You're too hyper. You're too ghetto. You're not going anywhere." Those were hurtful words, but I have forgiven most of the people who said them to me. It wasn't their fault their daddy's sperm hit the rottenest egg when he busted his nut. I forgive, but I do not forget. I've got the memory of an elephant when it comes to people who've wronged me. So here's what I do: When I've got a movie coming out, I call up my publicist and make sure my billboards go up in the neighborhoods where my biggest haters live so they have to look at my face smiling at them everywhere they turn. *You're right. I'm not going anywhere. I'm everywhere.* Then I take the mess they used to talk about me, use it in my act, and I make money off it. *How you like that shit?*

What's Up with Roscoe?

I have not seen Roscoe. It's one of the great losses in my life that I do not know where Roscoe is. I've decided he must be rotting in a coffin somewhere because I cannot find him. Ain't no way in hell he doesn't know I'm looking for him. I've told that story a million times. He's got to know I'd like to hear from him. If he isn't dead, then Roscoe's a dick. I kind of hope he's dead, so he's not out there breaking anybody else's heart. RIP, Roscoe.

How's Your Mom Doing?

I ain't going to lie; it's day by day. I did manage to get Mom out of the institution. I pour a lot of my money into getting her care. I try to get her the right foods, the chefs, the healers, everything I could possibly do, and to some degree, it is working. She's getting her body together. She lost a bunch of weight. She was full-blown diabetic a few years ago, now she's back to what the doctors call prediabetic, so that's good. I bought her a house like I had always wanted to do. But life isn't like the movies. There hasn't been a slow fade with "Lovely Day" playing in the background while we hold hands and smile at each other on the couch. Most days, she's still talking to herself or to people only she can see. She can get in a full argument with herself and be busting up laughing by the end. I try to find the funny in it. I tell myself, *My mom don't have to have friends. Her friends are in her head. She's never lonely!* Other times, it's tough to find the funny. I'll take her for a perfectly normal mother–daughter afternoon, but then something will set her off, and boom, she's trying to fight one of the employees wherever we're at or coming at me, trying to beat me up, scratch my eyes out.

I have to remind myself I am not God, so I should stop trying to be. I love her, but whew, it is still hard.

Why Aren't You Married Again Yet?

Mind your business.

Do You Still Use Groupon?

Hell yeah, I still use Groupon. I got more money than I used to when my ass was homeless, but I still know the value of a dollar. I use Groupon like a mofo. In the past year, I bought an electric toothbrush. A hundred fast-acting weight loss patches. A psychic reading. (That lady was bad. She was wrong about every damn thing. I gave her one star. But that reading was only ten dollars, so I guess you get what you pay for.) Six rhinestone face masks. A Galaxy lightweight jacket that came with holes in the pockets. (One star.) Dual pack of high-waisted women's shorts. Disposable extra-thick latex gloves. A padded sports bra. High-waisted bike yoga shorts. A lady's sexy three-fourth sleeve dress. Three-piece vinyl home gym kettlebells. (I've been working out.) And premium-strength biotin hair, skin, and nail patches. If you think I'm going to waste my hard-earned money paying retail, get out of here.

When Are You Going to Do *Girls Trip 2*?

Me and the girls talk about doing a sequel all the time. I would love for Meryl Streep to be in the movie and play my mama. If you've got ideas for that script, holla at your girl.

If You Did Not Read *The Last Black Unicorn* . . .

First of all, why the hell not? You don't even have to *read* it. You can get it as an audiobook and listen to it while you're brushing your teeth in the morning. I was nominated for a Grammy for my recording of the audiobook. I didn't know you could get nominated for a Grammy for reading. But I did. I got nominated for reading out loud when I didn't even learn to read until *high school*. How about that pot of beans?

Anyway, if you haven't read my first book, I am not going to spoil it for you, but there are some things I should tell you before you go on ahead and read *this* book because I refer to them and you might need a little background—a little context—to know where I'm coming from.

The bottom line is that I did not come out of my mama's vagina a famous comedian. My early life was like a Lifetime movie: *From the Hood to Hollywood: The Tiffany Haddish Story*. My journey was not the smoothest. There was heartbreak and drama and a lot of pain.

My daddy left our family before I turned four years old—just vanished, leaving my mom and grandma to raise me. We were doing all right until my mama got in a very serious car accident when I was eight years old. Her head went right through the windshield. She had been a businesswoman. She had properties. She wasn't a dumb woman. But after that accident, her mind just wasn't the same.

She was in the hospital for three months while I lived with my grandmother and my aunties. She had to learn to talk, walk, and eat all over again. Her doctor told me, "You have to grow up now, be her biggest helper."

"No problem," I told him. "I love her. No matter what she needs, I'll do it."

Her accident changed our dynamic, flipped it 180 degrees. At nine years old, I was like instant mom. Everything my mom had taught me, I had to teach her. I had to teach her to walk again and talk again. She had had a really big vocabulary before she got hurt, but afterward, she barely had any words. She couldn't express herself properly, which pissed her off, and she became very violent.

A few years later, the doctors diagnosed her with schizophrenia, but I feel like she had one of those football player concussions that give you mood swings. She would get so frustrated and emotional, she would bust me in the mouth. *Bam.* She mollywopped me. She clowned me. She broke my little spirit. I lost all the rest of my baby teeth at once. She even knocked me out a few times.

You should never have to fight your mama like that.

I lived in constant fear, trying to figure out how to avoid getting my neck broke or another tooth knocked out of my head. How could I make this person happy enough to not hurt me?

By the time I was thirteen, my brothers, sisters, and I ended up in foster care because I guess I wasn't that great of a mom. I lived in a few different homes.

As you can imagine, those lumps and bumps didn't make for the best environment for a young person. I was getting in trouble at school. A lot. My social worker gave me a choice between going to psychiatric therapy or enrolling in the Laugh Factory Comedy Camp. I chose comedy camp. It saved my life—emotionally and mentally— but it didn't put much food on the table or a roof over my head.

For a time in my twenties, my Geo Metro was my mobile home. I was homeless, but I was cute homeless. I didn't have a shower, but I had baby wipes to clean the important parts. My hair and nails were

always done. I was doing my thing—booking gigs, auditioning, trying to build up my career. I looked good, but I was still sleeping in
my car, hungry as fuck, counting the pennies in my ashtray to get
something to eat. Then, one blessed day, Kevin Hart confronted me
about being homeless. Instead of making me feel ashamed, he helped
me. That man is an angel to me.

Once I got back on my feet, I was able to focus on the thing that
saved my life—the thing that gives me meaning and joy and enough
money to eat and sleep in a real bed in my own house: comedy.

Okay, that's the basics. Most of the stories in this book will make
sense to you now. But, seriously, now that you have this book, go and
read my last one, too.

BRAVE NEW WORLD

THE FIRST BOOK I read cover to cover was Alex Haley's *Queen*. Reading it was my high school drama teacher's idea. Miss Gree was the teacher who busted me for being essentially illiterate at fifteen years old. I could pretty much only read three-letter words by that age, and I couldn't spell for shit. I thought "if" was spelled "ef." She had been making me visit her outside of class and read to her for practice. I'd come in and stumble through articles from the newspaper she'd picked out or parts of books for my class assignments. One afternoon in her classroom, she suggested I choose a book on my own, one that I might like. I had no idea where to begin, so Miss Gree asked me, "Well, how about this, then—what is your favorite movie that was based on a book?"

"I don't know."

"Okay, what's your favorite movie? Let's start there."

"That's easy. *Who Framed Roger Rabbit*." I loved that movie because there was a scene where the detective says, "Why are all these people doing these nice things for you?" And the rabbit says, "Because I make 'em laugh, Eddie. If you make 'em laugh, they'll do anything for you." Making people laugh was my go-to move to get them to help my illiterate ass with my schoolwork, but I guess there wasn't a book for *Roger Rabbit,* so that was off the table.

"Hmm," Miss Gree said, "why don't you think about it and come back to me?"

I thought about it, and what I came up with wasn't a movie. It was the television miniseries *Alex Haley's Queen.* The reason that was one of my favorites was because the day after the first episode aired, this boy Eugene at school had said to me, "Tiffany! Tiffany! Did you see *Queen* this weekend? Ohmigod. You look just like Halle Berry."

I said, "Thank you! She is so pretty."

"Yeah, you look like Halle Berry when she run down. Like dirty Halle Berry."

Damn. Why did he have to say I looked like a busted Halle Berry? Couldn't he have said I looked like Halle Berry out of *The Flintstones* movie or *Boomerang*? But you know what, hearing him say that still made me feel gorgeous because Halle Berry is incredibly beautiful, no matter what role she plays. Also, that miniseries was very good.

So, *Queen* was the book I wanted to read. I went to the school library to check it out, but they didn't have any copies. Me and my best friend, Lena, ended up going to the Inglewood Library to see if they had it.

For a girl who couldn't read so good, I spent a shit ton of time at the library. Because I moved around a lot from house to house growing up, it was the one place that felt stable. Same shelves. Same dusty book smell. Same homeless folks taking a nap at the table. Before I could read, I checked out books on tape. They came in those hard plastic packages. Even a short book was like fifty cassettes long, but I loved listening to them. I got so many stories for free. When I browsed the shelves, I hadn't been able to read all the titles. I could maybe sound out one or two words like "romance" or "rich." Any audiobook that said "rich" in it, I checked that out because I was planning to be rich myself one day. I was also a sucker for a sexy cover. *Oh, this one got a werewolf and a woman with her bosoms sticking out on it. Lemme get that.* I'd pop the tapes in my Walkman when I got home and be good for hours.

Looking for *Queen* was the first time I'd gone into the library to find a specific paper book. Lena and I got it off the shelf and checked it out. It was thick as hell. Must have been seven hundred pages. You could have used it as a step stool. The weight of it felt good in my hands.

Once I started reading *Queen*, I took that book with me every-where. I read it on the school bus. I read it on the regular bus. Sometimes, when someone talked smack on me and I got so mad I wanted to fight them, instead of swinging, I took *Queen* into a bath-room. I would pound the shit out of that big-ass book until my hand hurt. That was a new approach for me because, much as I hate to admit it, when I was young, my go-to for dealing with my emotions was to want to fight somebody. They didn't always want to fight me back because they thought I was nuts, so I would try to destroy them with my words. My mind was like an assault rifle firing off insults. But while I had *Queen* in my book bag, I put down my weapons. After I punched the cover for a while, I would sit down on the toilet and rage read. Reading about life on the plantation calmed me down, which is a pretty fucked-up thing to say, I guess. But the story was so absorbing, and the writing was fucking beau-tiful. It sucked me in so deep, it was like I was inside the characters, feeling whatever they felt—like when Queen was so desperate to know more about her father. Damn, I could relate to that, and that connection kept me turning page after page. The magic thing about reading was what this character was going through, close as it was to whatever I was going through in my own life, couldn't hurt me. The story was just words on a page, so I could let myself feel those feelings without getting drawn into a bad place. Pretty soon, I'd forget about whatever bullshit in my real life that was pulling me down.

So, that was the first book I ever finished that wasn't by Dr. Seuss. It took me forever to get through the whole thing. It's not easy to get through a full book when you are just past the Hooked on Phonics reading level. When I finally closed the cover, I was so proud. In fact, I was so proud, I never gave the book back to the library. I paid like $12.80 in fines, and I still have it on my shelf at home stamped on the bottom with "Inglewood Public Library." My bad.

The second book I read was *Brave New World* by Aldous Huxley. Now, that book was sexy as fuck—full of orgy porgies. The characters lived in this alternate universe where they could have all the sex they wanted. They didn't believe in marriage or monogamy, and there was no jealousy. They never felt any negative emotions at all because anytime they felt bad, they took these little pellets called soma that made them feel good, made them feel happy. As soon as you felt a bad emotion, you could take a pill. Gulp, then bam, it's gone. Y'all have to read this book. (Or not. It has some fucked-up white people politics in it, but I didn't pick up on any of that when I was a teenager.) I kept thinking the book was called *Utopia* because the world they were in seemed perfect to me.

In the book, they live in a place called the World State where the characters made babies in a Petri dish. They would grow them in this lab where everybody had their designated job. It was totally clear to everyone what was expected of them at all times and what their role was. Either they were in charge of fertilizing the egg or they determined what the child's rank would be in society once it was born. There was no guesswork about how you fit in. It was all worked out for you.

Outside the World State bubble was what they called the "Savage Reservation." (See what I mean about the politics? This book was obviously written a long time ago by a man who could have been elected mayor in the Jim Crow South. It's been a minute since I read it, but if there were Black characters in that book, I guarantee they were referred to as "negroes.") Anyway, this was a place very similar to how we live now: having babies naturally that come out of your vagina, falling in love with a partner, getting sick, aging—all the stuff we're used to dealing with. There's all these horrible emotions: disappointment, depression, anger—feelings that can stomp on your soul.

By the time I was in high school reading *Brave New World*, I'd had a lot of experience watching my mom struggle with her emotions. After her accident, they were all over the goddamn map. She was literally schizophrenic and probably had been for years, though the doctors didn't diagnose her until I was around twelve years old. That was four years of her being unmedicated and unpredictable. Her violence kicked up to its highest point after she lost a baby.

She'd been feeling sick, throwing up like she had the flu. I was bringing her tea and crackers, running to the corner store to try to get her food with our food stamps. I came back one day, and she was crying her eyes out in the bathroom. I asked her, "What's wrong, Mama?"

"I'm pregnant. I don't know what I'm going to do."

"What do you mean, you're pregnant? We don't have space for you to be pregnant. Why did you do that? Things are hard enough already."

I was so mad at her, so disappointed. I thought, *Here comes another kid I am going to have to take care of.*

When she learned it was twins, she was so damn happy. It had her smiling. Twins! What a blessing. But then, a month or two later when she was around four months, she lost one of the babies. It was like whatever happiness and calm she'd had died with that baby. She was so sad, moping around, not taking care of herself, not even showering. In her state of mind, she was so fucked up, she was muttering about how the doctors had snuck her some abortion pills and that's why the baby died.

The moment the surviving baby, my brother Justin, was born, all her emotions—the pain, the grief, the frustration—swallowed her up. She suffered from serious mental illness to the point where she didn't even want to feed the new baby. We didn't have money for Similac, so I would pick up my brother, smelling all musty, and wipe him down. I'd take him over to my mama and wipe down her titties and her armpits so she didn't stink, and then I'd put him on her titty so he'd have something to eat.

She didn't have energy for taking care of herself or her baby, but she did have energy to beat my ass. The violence kicked up times ten. It was like her emotions filled up her body to where it was going to burst, and the only way she could let them out was to hit me. It was straight-up scary. I had no idea who I'd be dealing with from moment to moment. I woke up every day wondering, *Am I going to have to fight my mama today?*

Who knows if her outcome would have been different if doctors had gotten her the help she needed earlier. All I know is those years sure would have been different for me.

After I started reading *Brave New World*, I would tell her, "Mama, you need to take some medicine. If you just popped some pills, you would be a much happier person."

The people who were taking their pills in that World State, they were happy. There was order because there were no intense emotions, no stormy relationships to rock the boat. When the characters were sucking those pills down, no one was punching their daughter in the face. Whenever my mom started swinging, the inescapable destiny of a predetermined world sounded pretty fucking good.

It wasn't long after Justin was born that the social workers started showing up at our house to check in on us to see how we were doing. The answer was: not good. They tried to get my mother to do a psych evaluation, but she refused. They tried to get her to consider medication, but she said, "I only want to take Herbalife. I don't like how pills make me feel." Finally, my mama snapped and got so violent she got herself arrested, and all of us kids ended up in foster care, which I talked about in my last book. The police took her to the hospital, and they sent her to a mental institution. At the institution, she finally got some drugs in her system to calm her down.

My grandma rounded up all the kids from our different homes to come visit my mom in the institution. When we got there, I could hardly recognize her. Whatever they had given her—Haldol, I think—it had knocked her out of herself. She had drool sliding down her face, and she was just moaning, "Huuuuuhhhhp," almost like she was saying "help." I hope you never have to see someone you love like that.

Fast-forward to my twenties, my life was not going well. If you know anything about me, then you probably know this story, so I'm not going to repeat it in a whole lot of detail. Let's just get to the point. I was making dumb decisions that left me broke, hungry, and living in my car. It was a low, hard time.

I had a full nervous breakdown. I was super depressed. The feelings I was having at that time were too much for me, and I just short-circuited. I didn't know which way to go, what to do with myself. There were days I flat-out wanted to die. I even ran a red light or two on purpose.

I went to therapy, though I wasn't a natural as a patient. Instead of talking about what was wrong with me, I would run material in my therapist's office. She'd sit on her chair across from me, barely able to take notes 'cause she was laughing so hard. I was paying this bitch $125 an hour so I could do stand-up on her couch. We weren't making a lot of progress. Talking alone wasn't cutting it, so I told her I needed something stronger than our sessions. She referred me to a psychiatrist who prescribed me medication. I thought, *All right, now we're getting somewhere. I'll take these pills, and that will make all the pain go away. Sign me up.*

I started with Paxil. First thing that happened was it dried me up. Soon as I started taking those pills, my mouth went dry. My lips were always parched. My feet were cracked. And my vagina was chafing. Do you know how hard it is to walk fast when your coochie is dry? You ever see an older lady try to cross the street? All curled up like a shrimp. You gotta walk slow 'cause if you rub your walls together too fast, your coochie's just gonna blow up. It was uncomfortable. I had no juices. I drank water, so much water, but I was still so dry. All my tears had dried up, too, but I didn't even want to cry. I didn't feel sadness. I didn't feel anger. I didn't feel joy. I didn't feel *anything*. Except the need to yawn. I was yawning all the fucking time.

So then I switched to Prozac. I did get some moisture back in my mouth. There was no more yawning. I still felt nothing—like *nothing*. Absolutely nada.

Everything that used to give me pleasure didn't anymore. I didn't even care about eating. Food tasted like wet paper. You could have served me the best meal in the world, and I would enjoy it as much as instant oatmeal. I didn't feel like hanging out with my friends. Nothing had changed about them. They were still the same people I had loved for years, but when they'd call me to ask if I wanted to chill, I felt the same amount of excitement I would have if I was talking to someone who'd called to sell me insurance. It was like someone took a ratchet and cranked my joy valve shut.

Even though I felt like shit, I was killing it onstage because that was the one place I had always been able to connect to my feelings, and even the pills didn't totally kill that. A good show could still give me an adrenaline rush, and I knew I should feel happy that I was getting gigs, but I just didn't. I felt empty. Weirdly, I was smiling a lot more with the Prozac, but there was nothing genuine about those smiles. My face was just responding to the idea "I should be smiling now," not a feeling of happiness in my heart.

It was like my heart was turned off. To try to jump-start it, I started fucking everything under the sun because I just wanted to feel something. To be fair, I did feel something, but what I felt was pain. Sex would *hurt*. My vaginal area, my root chakra, was not working. There was no energy flowing down there. Sex was a purely mechanical act. Dudes could get it in, but I wasn't having orgasms. After a night of bad sex, I'd think, *Okay, maybe I'm connecting with the wrong guy. Maybe this is not the right person. Let me try another.* And I'd go find me a new man to mess around with. But nope. Still nothing.

I was all *feelinged* out. These pills were having the exact effect I'd wanted for my mom when, as a teenager, I tried to get her to take her pills, to shrink her feelings so small they wouldn't come bursting out of her fists and into my face. But what I was learning was that, in its own fucked-up way, no feelings was just as bad as too many.

Around that time, a lot of friends of mine were dying, getting killed in these gang wars and shit. You'd think I'd have felt some kind of way about that, but instead, I'd be like, "Wow, they are dead. Let us go to the funeral." Like a damn robot.

I was going to so many funerals. I was in such a messed-up mindset that I started to think they were the perfect place to pick up guys. At one service, I can't even remember whose it was, I homed in on this dude. He wasn't even that fine, but he was really tall. He had braids, and he was kind of funny. Andre, I think his name was.

He was looking sad at the ceremony. I got near him, pushed up all close, and started talking to him, saying things like, "I know. I know, it's so tragic. It's going to be okay." I stuck by him during the reception. We ate plates of macaroni and cheese and hung out the whole time. After that funeral, we started calling each other on the phone talking about this and that, getting to know each other. Before long, we were going out on dates and things got sexy.

One night over dinner, he set down his fork.

"I have to tell you something," he said. He finished chewing. "I got a big old dick."

I thought, *That ain't shit to me. I can take any dick. Little dick, big dick, it don't matter.*

"That's no problem. I can handle it. There ain't no dick that big. If God made it, then it's supposed to be that way. My body is built to stretch and shrink. That don't scare me."

He smiled so wide I thought he was going to ask me to marry him right there.

A few days later, we got together, and we started making out. It was clear we were gonna fuck. We moved into the bedroom and when he pulled it out, I froze. This motherfucker was bigger than a prize squash. He had a full-on baseball bat between his legs.

"Ohmigod. Look what you messing with!"

"I told you it was big."

I should have grabbed my drawers and been like, "Oh, shoot! I forgot I left my laundry in the machine. Gotta go!" But I had been talking so much about how I could handle any dick, I thought I had to back my shit up. Because I'm a woman of my word. I was so divorced from reality, I wasn't thinking about what a dick that big might do to the inside of me.

I excused myself, saying, "I'll be right back." I went to the bathroom and pulled some lube out of my purse. Normally, I'd just put a dollop on the outside of my coochie, but I put a good half of the tube way up in there for this dude. I was like, *I got to make sure she ready for this.*

I took a few deep breaths and then went back where he and his Louisville Slugger were waiting and got back to it. After some kissing, he put the tip in. I'm telling you, I was about to die. But did I cry? Nope. Did I run? Nope. Did I think about what I was doing?

Nope. I wasn't even in my body. I was floating somewhere above the whole scene watching it go down.

After he was done, Andre was so happy I thought he was going to get up and dance around the room. He said, "This the first time anybody let me put my whole thing in." No shit.

Wasn't five minutes after we finished up that I started having terrible pain in my abdomen, like there was a badger in there trying to chew its way out. I started throwing up—and throwing up and throwing up. I walked out of his bathroom all bent over.

"You feeling sick?"

"Yeah, my stomach is hurting really bad. Maybe it's something we ate?"

He dropped me off at home where I did not get much sleep 'cause that badger was fucking hungry. The next morning, I was in so much pain I could barely see. I kept throwing up even though there wasn't a damn thing left in my stomach. I got a little scared. *This motherfucker done gave me the herpesgonorrheasyphilis.*

I went to the hospital where the doctor did a pelvic exam, which was hard because I was so raw and swollen down there.

The doctor looked up from behind the sheet and said, "Your uterus is tilted."

That's how big Andre's dick was. It tilted my insides.

She said I had to massage myself and do Kegels to get my uterus back in place. That right there was when a seed was planted somewhere in my consciousness. I thought, *I need to get off these pills.*

"You're going to have to refrain from having sex for a while, and when you do it with this guy, you have to take it easy."

She didn't need to worry about that. I might have been numb to the world, but I wasn't stupid. I was not about to have sex with Long Dong Silver again.

A year later, I ran into Andre while he was with another woman. He introduced me to her, saying, "This is my wife."

I shook her hand and I'm sure I introduced myself, but all I could think was, *Girl, you a strong woman. You must have a coffee can for a vagina.*

It took me like maybe six weeks after that doctor's visit before I hooked up with somebody else. When I did, I didn't feel a damn thing in my coochie. It was numb. I thought Andre had permanently broken my vagina. Then I hooked up with another dude like a week later, and I was very glad I finally felt a little something down there—but I still didn't feel anything in my heart.

The Prozac was working too well. Numbing my pain was not working for me. I needed to get off those drugs. I was like one of those characters in Huxley's book. I was not really in the real world. I was in an artificial environment. There were no highs and no lows. My emotional landscape was a desert with no landmarks to ground me. I would have even welcomed a low, a prick of pain to wake me up to the fact that things weren't all bad all the time. If you never feel any pain, how can you know what joy feels like? I was feeling a whole lot of nothing. Pure flatness. I missed the big peaks and valleys of feeling. It was freaking awful. I realized a world without feelings isn't utopia; it's a dystopia, a nightmare that can destroy you.

I know a lot of people have been helped by antidepressants, and I don't want to tell anyone not to take something that is helping them, but those pills did not agree with me. I don't remember the exact day I took my last pill. I just know that I had decided, *No more.*

Once I stopped taking Prozac, it took maybe two or three days and then boom. I had a rush of feelings. All these different emotions crashed through me. A tidal wave of feelings. The juices were *back.* I let myself feel every sensation inside and out. It was such a relief. Like when you almost get into a car crash, but you swerve at the last minute, and you're suddenly so aware of how close you were to not existing and life goes Technicolor on you. I was sobbing, laughing randomly, feeling bouts of joy, bouts of super sadness. I had so much juice going through me, I didn't know what to do with it. When I was a teenager and my emotions threatened to take over, my impulse had been to beat some ass. I had tried turning off my feelings with pills. But once I quit them, I needed a new outlet. I decided, *Okay, when I feel like this, instead of swinging on somebody or taking a pill, I'm going to dance.* Every time I felt wild, I either cried or I danced. I danced when there was so much emotional energy flowing through me that I just needed to move. I cried when I was happy. I cried when I was sad. I mostly tried to do it in the shower unless I was really drunk, just me sobbing with God.

It's good for you to cry. You've got to remember, you were born crying. It was your first form of communication. You're squeezing everything you can't hold inside you anymore out your eyeballs. Every time I cried, it was like I was cleaning myself out. Sometimes, stuff came out that I didn't even know was in me. It was like I was a hoarder, but I didn't know it. I opened up a closet and, whoosh, everything I'd shoved in there fell out on top of me. At least now I could see what I was working with. Memories I'd suppressed tumbled out for me to sort through. I let myself feel those emotions instead of trying to shut them down.

Recently, I found this place called Break Room LA. It's a big warehouse where you can go and break stuff. They let you throw glasses up against the wall, smash plates on the floor, freaking break barrels, and bang metal with a sledgehammer. It is such a release. Afterward, I feel like I just had some of the best sex ever. They should open rage rooms like that in every city.

I let myself feel my feelings—all of them—instead of trying to stamp them out with medication or push them down or deny them. You don't get to feel the full force of the good emotions if you don't let yourself feel the bad ones.

I wear my heart on my sleeve for sure. The way I deal with heartache now is feeling the pain, embracing it, then making it part of my work and creativity. My emotions are fuel for my comedy. I chew up my pain, and bring it into me, so I can metabolize it and spit it out funny. I turn my pain into other people's joy, and that brings *me* joy. I might not know what it is I'm feeling all the time—'cause sometimes that shit is confusing—but I try not to get in the way of the full range of my emotions. When you're trying to fight it, if you suppress what you're feeling, you never know what other way it might come out or how you might be putting yourself in danger.

So, I let my feelings flow. I express them out loud. I have no problem saying, "I'm sad today, y'all." Some days, my feelings are so big, it's hard for me not to have snot flying out my nose. But I don't mind. Those big feelings are what make me human. They make me real. And they make me feel beautiful. Like Halle Berry.

SEX ED

WHEN I WAS A teenager and my social worker used to ask me what I wanted to be when I grew up, I would tell her, "I want to be something that is going to change other people's lives, like a nurse—or maybe I want to be someone who makes beef jerky because beef jerky is my favorite thing to eat." Now that I'm older, I have different career ambitions. I still want to change lives, but these days I think if this comedy thing doesn't work out for me, I'm going to get a job teaching sex ed. I would be so good at it! Everybody who came out of my class would leave it healthy because I'd teach them everything they needed to know. They wouldn't get diseases and they would be loving sex; it'd be so good for those kids to have all the information they need. They wouldn't have to be embarrassed because they didn't know what was up. Life is hard enough without people making you feel bad about things you don't know. Think about it. If you had someone who could be genuine and 100 with you about sex, you could have a nice, healthy sex life as opposed to being punked and bullied into things you don't want to be involved in or feeling like your body isn't good enough or any of the other things that come from having the wrong kind of experiences teach you about sex.

The way they teach health class right now is messed up. They don't tell you anything you actually need to know. There are so many things I had to learn through trial and error that I wish somebody would have told me so I would have been prepared. Like, they don't tell you that the reason your face is all bumpy is because you are stressed. Whenever I see some acne on someone's face, I think, *Oh, that person got a lot of stress and hormonal imbalance going on.* You ever met a teenager? They're fucked up. They've got a lot of issues on the inside they don't talk about.

Teenage years are some of the hardest because everything is changing and you have no control over it. Your body metamorphoses overnight. Your body's like, *Buddabuddabudda BOOBS! Budumbadumbadum BUTT!* Plus, you're going through emotions like one of those quick-change artists. One minute you love everything—*Ohmigod, drama club is the best!* Then, ten seconds later, you can't stand it—*Man, fuck drama club.*

Your teachers should talk you through all that—tell you everything you need to know about your emotions and your body, especially what happens to it during sex—but they don't. For example, no health educator in the history of the world has ever told their class about queefing. That shit takes you by surprise. The first time I experienced the thunder from down under, I was doing it doggie style with a dude who had a nice-size thang-thang. In my head, I was all, *Oh, this amazing. He's hitting from the back, and it's so good. I don't have to look at him or nothing.* I was raised up on my tippy toes like a black swan while my dude was back there pumping away. Then I heard it, that *pbbbbffffffft* sound. *What the fuck?* What was going on? Did something pop? He was big, but he wasn't *that* big. I didn't know what to do 'cause no one had told me about queefing. I didn't know whether to get up and run out of there real quick or bust up laughing.

He didn't miss a beat. In fact, he pumped even faster, like that coochie fart was a turn-on, so I just buried my face in my pillow like an ostrich and got back to fucking.

I simply did not know to expect a big old *pbbbbffffffffffffft* as a possibility because no one had sat me down in health class and gone, "Ladies, there will come a time when you're having sex and a man will be penetrating your vagina. As he's doing that, he'll be pumping air in there. Once you relax, a noise may come out that sounds a little something like this [*whoopee cushion*]. Don't be alarmed. It's natural. You're just relaxing." None of your girlfriends tell you either. They're not like, "Girl, I was doing it to Hector yesterday and, whew, honey child, he had my coochie beatboxing." If I taught sex ed, I'd tell people about that. And I'd let them know that some men love when the cookie is talking to them.

My own start with sex education was not the best because my mom was the first person to tell me about the birds and the bees when I was seven years old.

We were watching a soap opera one day, and the characters were kissing in the bed and getting into it. I looked at the bodies wriggling around each other on TV and then I looked at my mom and asked, "What are they doing, Mama?"

"That's what people do to make babies."

I thought about it a minute and said, "Then I'm going to do that one day." 'Cause back then, I wanted to have a mess of kids.

My mom didn't even take her eyes off the screen. She just said, "Nuh-uh. You can't be kissing no boys until you get your shot."

"My shot?"

She told me that I had to wait until I turned twenty-one to get with a boy because that's when you get your vaccine. She said boys have these enzymes in their mouths, and if you kiss them before you've been vaccinated, the enzymes will eat your face up. Then they will eat your throat up, and you will die within twenty-four hours.

The enzymes in a boy's mouth are dangerous until you get your vaccine. I was still trying to figure out what "enzymes" were when she said, "You get that vaccination and you won't get the sperm disease."

"The sperm disease? What's that?"

My mom sat back on the couch and told me how boys have this stuff that shoots out of their pee-pee hole. It looks like snot, and you never want to let that get on you and most definitely not inside you because it will eat up your baby carriage. Then your legs will fall off. And you'll die a slow, painful death in three days. I believed that craziness for a *long* time.

Soon after that first sex ed lesson from my mom, my family moved out of South Central to Pomona, and I had to go to a white school where they put me in Miss Takeuchi's class for second grade. That school was like 99.9 percent white, but there was this one other Black girl in Miss Takeuchi's class. I eventually became friends with another girl named Amber. Me and Amber were super cool. We would walk to school together every day and talk about this boy we both had a crush on named Ian. Ian did not like either one of us at first. He would not give us the time of day. But I guess Amber wore him down because one day I turned around and, all of a sudden, they were boyfriend and girlfriend. I wasn't mad. If he wasn't going to be with me, he might as well be with my best friend. Besides, I wanted Amber to be happy. But one afternoon, I saw Amber kiss Ian behind the school, and I instantly started crying—not because I was jealous but because I thought Amber was going to die from the kissing enzymes. I cried so hard, snot ran out my nose and down my shirt.

I ran over to her and grabbed her by the wrist.

"Amber, oh my God! You're going to die!"

"What are you talking about?"

I told her what my mama told me.

Amber rolled her eyes. "Tiffany, your mama don't know what she saying. That's not true."

But my mama had been very clear about that kissing disease, so I told her, "Amber, I care about you a lot. You my bestest friend, so I want you to know I'm going to be there at your funeral."

I was still crying when I got home. When my mom saw the tears and snot all over my face, she asked, "What you crying about? What's wrong?"

I did some of those shuddery breaths. "Amber kissed a boy and she gone die tomorrow. I don't even know why she did that. I told her, 'Don't kiss him,' and she kissed him anyway. She gownnnnana diiiiiiiie."

My mom shook her head and said, "Tiffany, you ain't got nothing to worry about. Amber's not going to die."

I stopped my sniveling for a second. "How do you know?"

"Because her family got the shot for her early. They knew she was going to be a ho."

I guessed that made sense? I mean, I didn't think my best friend was a ho, but I didn't know what went on in her parents' minds. So, okay, maybe she had had the shot and she didn't remember. I pulled myself together.

"Mom, I want to get the shot early, too, then."

"No way. You're not getting the shot early. Because you not a ho. We don't have hos in this family. You going to wait until you turn twenty-one."

I just said, "Okay." I was so relieved my friend wasn't going to die and have to have a closed casket 'cause her face had been all eaten up. For years after that, I was running around thinking people were out there getting vaccinated for the kissing enzymes and the sperm disease. When I saw people who were definitely not twenty-one yet kissing and humping, I'd go, "She a ho, that's a ho, she a ho, he a ho. That's a ho. Ho, ho, ho, ho."

My mom's accident happened soon after our discussion when I was eight. My worries about the sperm disease took a back seat for a while. Enzymes didn't seem so bad when your mom can't talk or remember who the fuck you are.

After a while, when my mom could talk again, we moved back to LA where I did have an actual sex education class in elementary school. The boys sat on one side of the auditorium; the girls sat on the other side. But they only taught us about periods (the vagina has a lining, then a bunch of blood comes out, and you have to wear these diapers called maxi pads) and very clinical stuff about sex itself (the sperm goes in the egg, and that's how you get pregnant). The end. They didn't go into detail about what the changes in our bodies would be like for us. When my breasts first came in, I thought I was getting breast cancer because the first little knots on my chest were so hard.

I was visiting with my grandma one day and she asked me, "How you doing? What's going on?"

I said, "Well, I'm pretty sure I got breast cancer."

"What? Why do you think you have breast cancer, Tiffany?"

"Because my chest hurts. My nipples hurt real bad, and there's a hard knot behind them."

"Oh, you got bee stings?"

"No, I didn't say anything about no bees. I'm telling you, I probably got breast cancer. I seen the thing in school, and it was talking about lumps. I got those lumps."

"You don't got no damn breast cancer. You're developing. Them is bee stings. You're going to have breasts."

Our sex ed teachers had never mentioned that your breasts might feel hard at first. It was like they'd wanted to blast through the facts as fast as they could without getting into the specifics, especially about girls' bodies.

Actually, there was a lot the teachers didn't mention in those classes. When they were telling us about sex, they didn't say that sperm comes out of his pee-pee hole and looks like snot, so I didn't make the connection to what I thought I knew about sex.

In junior high school, we had more health classes, but it was the same thing—all very theoretical. Nothing about it seemed real or connected to actual human bodies. And it definitely did not seem pleasurable. It seemed like science. By eighth-grade health class, we finally got to the nitty-gritty. We were talking about *all* the sex stuff: the mechanics, the hormones, the STDs. I thought, *Okay, all right. Here we go. We about to learn about the sperm disease.* I was listening my ass off, all right. But the first couple days of STD week went by, and there was no mention of the sperm disease. What the hell?

I kept waiting for our teacher, Mr. Thill, to describe something that sounded like the sperm disease. I thought maybe my mama hadn't known the proper name for it, maybe it was called something else—*spermatcus enzymus* or something. Then, toward the end of the week, we were wrapping up the unit, and he said, "And that's all the diseases you can get. Moving on . . ." I put my hand up in the air.

"Mr. Thill! Mr. Thill! Yo, you forgot the most important one. What about the sperm disease?"

He looked at me like, *Huh?*

"You know, the sperm disease? You didn't say anything about the sperm disease."

"What is the sperm disease, Tiffany? Explain this to me."

So I told him what I knew. I went into the whole thing. I talked about the enzymes, the face eating, the dying, the vaccine we were all going to get. The whole class went stone silent.

When I was done, Mr. Thill asked, "Who told you that, Tiffany?"

"My mom."

He looked real thoughtful. "How long have you been at this school?"

"This is my second year here."

"Have you seen people kissing?"

"Yeah, I seen people kissing. I definitely seen people kissing, but we know they already got the vaccine. They hos! They mama got it for them early. I haven't been vaccinated. I have to wait until I turn twenty-one."

Mr. Thill sort of shook his head. "I would suggest you go home and have a conversation with your mother."

Everybody in the class busted up laughing. I looked at them like they were dumb as hell.

Maybe I should have known by then. Maybe there should have been a moment where I'd sat my mom down and asked, "Were you messing with me about this sperm disease or what?" The thing was, I couldn't actually talk to my mom about it. After her accident, the last thing I wanted to talk to her about was sex. By the time Mr. Thill told me I should have another sex talk with her, I wasn't even around my mom that much anymore because I'd gone into the foster care system earlier that year. I was not about to bring up sex with my foster mom and give her an excuse to throw me out of the house. Instead, I brought the whole discussion up to my social worker. I laid it all out for her and told her everything my mom had told me about sex and how Mr. Thill didn't seem to know what I was talking about. I asked her could she please clear things up for me.

"Well, Tiffany," she said, "I can't say that your mother was right. And I'm not going to say she's wrong. Because there *are* germs . . ."

It was as if she didn't want to ruin a potentially good thing. She was like, *I see the value in what your mom was doing there. It was a little misguided, but at least you not a ho.*

"But what I will tell you is that you want to make sure you know whoever it is you're going to be intimate with. Kissing is very intimate."

That started me thinking I should probably learn how to kiss a boy so I wouldn't fuck it up when I got around to it after I got that vaccine. My girl Lena, who I'd met when I was twelve, and I started practicing how to kiss all the time. She would show me.

"This how you got to learn how to kiss. You get a ponytail holder and put it up to your lips and go like, *ehhhh ehhh ehhh*." She'd hold up a ponytail holder and move her mouth all around inside like she was kissing it.

There was this girl Tanya who was fourteen, a whole year older than us, who saw us practicing our kissing on the bus and she said, "No, that's not going to work. What you got to do is practice on the back of your hand like this [*mimes smacking on her hand*]."

So Lena and I would practice slobbering on the back of our hands all the way home. Tanya would watch us like she was our coach.

"No, you're giving too much tongue. Less tongue, less tongue. He got to give all the tongue."

A few weeks later, we saw Tanya kissing a boy in the lower C building that ran beneath the first floor where you entered the school. That's where all the freaky stuff went down, where kids went to smoke weed or put their hands down each other's pants. Then, like a week later, we saw her kissing a whole 'nother boy on the quad. I said, "Oh shoot, Lena, Tanya fixing to be dead. She better had got the vaccine. She gonna die." Lena's face went, *You really believe that shit you said to Mr. Thill?* Then she looked me square in the eye.

"Tiffany, you stupid." She gave it to me. "Girl, your mama lied to you. I done kissed a bunch of boys, and I ain't got no disease vaccine. You not going die. Ain't nothing going happen to you. Only thing that will happen to you is if they put they pee-pee in you, you gonna get pregnant. That's it."

Well, now. What was I supposed to do with that information? Lena was my ride-or-die. I trusted her more than any teacher. I knew she wouldn't lie to me. We were always straight with each other, so I started wondering if maybe my mama was wrong after all.

"Okay, maybe you right. But I still want to know why Tanya is kissing so many boys."

The next day, we asked Tanya why she was kissing on so many different dudes.

"I'm just trying to become a better kisser. You got to kiss a few boys, and *that's* how you really become a good kisser. You just copy what they do. Whatever he do, that's what you do."

If Lena had kissed a bunch of dudes and Tanya had kissed a bunch of dudes and they both still had all their skin, maybe no enzymes were going to gobble up my face if I kissed somebody. Interesting. I'd have to chew on that.

By the time me and Lena were fresh off the summer of ninth grade, I was pretty sure there was no such thing as the sperm disease. Maybe it was time for me to try some kissing. Besides, I figured, *Life has been going pretty bad. I'm in foster care. My mom's crazy. If I get eaten alive, that's fine with me. At least I will have kissed a boy.*

The boy I had in mind for my first kiss, Jerome, looked like a damn werewolf. He was ug-a-ly. For real, a straight-up boogawolf. But that boogawolf was always looking at me out of the side of his eyes when I walked by his desk, so I knew he liked me. I just didn't know if I liked him. I told Lena I wasn't sure if I was going to go through with my plan to make him my first kiss. She said, "Tiffany, they ain't all gon' be perfect. You got to start somewhere."

"I don't know. He a dog."

"But he like you. Don't nobody else like you." Girl had a point.

I was hanging out at Jerome's house one afternoon. We were sitting around listening to Babyface and he smelled nice, like Irish Spring soap, so I went for it. I brought my face in close to his and pushed our lips together. I was doing it! I was finally kissing a boy! I got to say, his kiss was pretty gross. He moved his mouth around so much, it was like he was trying to eat up my face. Like the enzymes! He stuck his tongue down my throat, all *uhhh, uhhh, uhhh.* I remembered what Tanya had said, so I did it right back. *Uhhh, uhhh, uhhh.* After a while, he said, "Wow, you're an amazing kisser." We made out for probably an hour. I do not know if it was his slobber or my mom's warning bouncing around deep in the back of my brain that was keeping me from enjoying myself, but I did not like the kissing. I rolled with it, though. Like Lena said, I had to start somewhere.

When I got home, I looked in the mirror. My face was all still there—lips, teeth, cheeks, everything. No sign of the enzymes. How about that?

I know that sounds like a long time to wait before I learned that I wasn't going to die from sex or have my face eaten from kissing. You might think I'm embarrassed about that, but I'll tell you something. I'm not. Not at all. I'm not embarrassed because I didn't know. In my opinion, you should not be embarrassed about something you don't know. There's a lot of things to know in this world, and nobody is born knowing them all—or any of them, really. Babies got to be shown how to do everything but breathe and shit. You have to learn pretty much everything else by living.

If I don't have the information, I just got to figure it out as best I can or 'til somebody teaches me different. I know some people will do anything they can not to look ignorant. They act like they know everything. Who are you trying to fool, fool? If someone asks me something I don't know, I don't pretend I know it. What's the point of that? Someone will say, "You know this famous artist or that actor or some businessperson?" Instead of dancing around trying to hide that I don't know what they're talking about or changing the subject, I'll just go, "Nope. Who's that?"

Recently, I was doing a live show, and there were some technical difficulties when I was introducing someone. The producers came over my earpiece and started telling me to "vamp" to kill time until they could get us up and running again. What now? I went, *I don't know what vamp mean. "Vamp" sounds like it means become a vampire or e-vamp-orate, like disappear. How am I gonna disappear?*

Maybe they mean elaborate? I could do that. But instead of fronting like I knew what they were talking about, I just fessed up on the air what was happening—someone was telling me to "vamp," and I had no fucking idea what that was. I was not embarrassed. We recovered, and the show went on. Nobody died. Sky didn't fall. And I learned a new word. (Also, vamp? Who says "vamp"? If they had just said "improvise," we would have been golden.)

Never feel ashamed of not knowing something 'cause ain't nobody perfect and nobody knows everything. We're in these meat suits to learn what other people have to teach us and what we can figure out for ourselves. If you are scared of looking stupid, that kills your curiosity and then you never learn anything new.

That said, I wish someone had told me the real deal about sex before I actually had sex. If I had known what it was all about, I might have enjoyed it more from the get-go. It's like when you go to a restaurant and there's a bunch of items you don't recognize on the menu. If you don't speak up and ask what *unagi* is (because someone told you all sushi is basically the same), you might choke on the boney piece of eel that ends up on your plate. But if you could get over the shame of feeling like maybe you don't have all the information you need and ask, "What the fuck is that?"—or better yet, if the restaurant had a good translation printed on the menu—then you could order something you might actually enjoy.

Who knows? Maybe someday I will go to school to learn how to be an actual sex ed teacher. If that ever happens, I'm going to answer every single question those kids have. I'll tell them the unvarnished truth about sex, and then I'll end every class with something my character Mia says in *Like a Boss*: Be safe—and if you're not safe, name it after me.

IF YOU WANT TO GET WITH ME

I HAVE A REPUTATION for being very open about what goes on in my sex life. Probably the thing I'm most famous for was when I demonstrated how to give a blowjob like Auntie Angel using a banana pushed through the center of a grapefruit in *Girls Trip*. I went to town on that fruit, licking and sucking like a pro. Everyone started getting their vitamin C with their vitamin D after that scene hit the screens because grapefruit sales went through the roof.

I don't consider myself a dirty comic, but I am not afraid to say "pussy" in public. I'm 100 percent comfortable talking about my vagina onstage or even putting it to work. Not like that. I'm no pay-to-play ho, but there was one time at the Laugh Factory where somebody called out for me to queef onstage, and I did it on demand. Just let one rip out over the crowd. The noise resonated through the whole club like someone had stepped on a goose. Everybody freaking lost it. This woman with long braids who'd been sitting way in the back came up to me afterward and said, "No way that sound came out of you. You must have some kind of machine in your pocket. Where is it?" But no. I just did it natural because my body is an amazing machine.

If you listen to me perform, you might get the idea that I am, shall we say, promiscuous. I have definitely been out here in these streets, and I am not going to deny that I do have a certain amount of experience. If you are looking to hit it with somebody brand-new, look elsewhere. But if you want somebody who knows her body, knows how she wants it, and knows how to make sure everyone has a good time, then hop on top!

I will not just get with any old dick, though. There are certain standards a dude has to meet. If you want to get with me, here's what's up.

You've Got to Put in the Work

If we ever really wanted to make a big change in society—get rid of systemic racism, eliminate poverty, fix healthcare, etcetera—the way to do it would be for women to stop having sex. Just close our legs. Shut our fun factories down. No more coochie. I'm telling you, wars would end. If every woman just said, "I'm putting this punani on lock until justice is served, until we have world peace, and until everyone has enough to eat. You are not getting any more of this unless you march your ass down to the polling place and vote up some social justice," two months later, we'd be all fixed up 'cause dudes will do damn near anything if they think there is a chance they are going to fuck.

For example, in my twenties, I used to bring guys to my apartment and make them color before they could fuck me. You heard me right. Grown-ass men—gangbangers, dope dealers, police—they would come in my house, and I would throw down a princess coloring book or *Toy Story* coloring book and some markers on my kitchen table and say, "Look, you trying to get with me? I'm gonna need you to color some unicorns. Make it real beautiful. If it looks really great, I'll fuck the shit out of you. If it looks sloppy, all out of the lines, wack colors, then you wack and I ain't effing with you." Then I'd check his work because you can tell a lot by how someone colors. Was he taking creative liberties—pink leaves on the trees and a purple sun in the sky? Was I going to end up upside down in a big-ass Afro wig? Or was he inside the lines and by the book? Lights out, missionary only? Either way, I wanted to see what I was dealing with.

And you know what? Only three dudes refused to color for me. I found out later two were gay.

I like you to show me you're willing to do whatever it takes to get me naked, so get to work.

Get to Know Tiffnicity

I have talked about my vagina so much you could do a police sketch of it. (I call her Tiffnicity. Tiffnasty, if you're nasty.) That drawing wouldn't be pretty because when I talk about my vagina, it's not necessarily in the best light. I'm not over here saying my coochie's a beautiful orchid with delicate petals or a soft velvet purse that will envelop you and make you talk to angels. Instead, I've said that my pussy tastes like garlic chicken and looks like a hot dog that exploded from being in the microwave too long.*

So, the sketch might not look the best. But you still have to get to know her if you want to be with me. You got to get up inside Tiffnicity and find my G spot, memorize that location, and drop a pin on your sex GPS.

One of these days, I'm gonna teach a class on how to find the G spot. There's going to be quiet music tinkling as I take people on a journey of

---

* To be clear, I do not hate my vagina. My vagina is my girl. I love her. She does not look like a blown-up hot dog. That was a *joke*. If anything, she looks like the bottom of a nice healthy slug.

self-discovery. I personally got familiar with every inch inside of myself during a bunch of lonely nights in my thirties. I smoked a little weed and got to know Tiffnicity real intimately. I touched around in there—*Hey, girl. What you about?*—pushing on all the soft and squishy bits, but not much happened for a while except my fingers got sticky. It was nothing, nothing, nothing, and then, *Oh, hold up now, what's that? Well, now, this is an interesting sensation.* My sex life leveled up after that because I learned how to move my body to get what I needed.

I wish I had known where my spot was in my twenties. I wouldn't have wasted so much time with these donkey dicks. (For the record, my G spot is three inches in and to the left. The rest is just living space.) Now that I found where to press, I can take care of myself whenever I want in about three minutes, so you had best make it worth my time to let you in there.

I Don't Need a Power Hour

I want to be intimate with you for about twenty-five minutes total, with actual sex for only about five to seven of those minutes, then I want to go to sleep for around fifty hours. I'm not into kissing for a long time. I do not need you to clean my whole face with your tongue like you're a mama cow. After more than thirty seconds or a minute of making out, I'm thinking, *What are you waiting for? Fucking take my clothes off already.*

Once we're really going at it, it doesn't take much to get me over the line. Get it in the right spot six, seven, eight times, I'm good. Much more than that, and I'm wondering, *What's going on? Am I getting a pelvic exam? Is this a hysterectomy?*

And do not try to surprise me with some bullshit you saw on Pornhub. If you are thinking about busting out something extraordinary, you better talk to me about it first 'cause if you don't, I will turn around and punch you. Like, I got a neck issue. Don't kiss my neck, don't lick my neck, don't touch my neck. Even if you come near my neck to whisper things in my ear, I might pop you. You gotta let me know what's happening. Ask before you come in my neck space.

Some men want you to tell them how they can make you feel good, and I'm happy to oblige. *Here you go. I printed out some IKEA picture instructions for you. Three easy steps, no tools required.* But then other guys want to go on a two-hour adventure to explore your body. They want you to be more mysterious, to lay clues for them, giving them little hints like, "To valley yonder thy lips should wander. If to the left you wind, a magical world ye shall find." Motherfucka, I don't have time for a treasure hunt. I'm a busy woman. I told you where my G spot is. Just get to it.

Do Not Show Me That Thing

I'm going to tell you right now: Unless I ask to see it, you shouldn't be pulling your dick out of your drawers. If you're showing it to me within five minutes of our date starting, I'm immediately asking myself who else you've been showing your dick to.

The worst first date I've ever been on was when I was twenty-three. I went out with this dude who was very handsome, light skin, light eyes, couple pockmarks on his cheeks, very fit. He picked me up in his Jeep Wrangler. Nelly was shaking the speakers, and I could hear him as soon as he pulled up in front of my house. I opened the door, brushed some KitKat wrappers off the passenger seat, and climbed in the car. When I put my purse on the floor, my thermos banged into my ankle. This was back when I used to bring my own drink to a restaurant to let my date know I was considerate and liked to save money. I'd bring a little thermos with vodka in it. The waiter would come, and I'd just ask for some three-dollar cranberry juice.

We hadn't even gotten to the restaurant yet—we were still in the car stopped at a stoplight—when I smelled something funny . . . like a baloney sandwich. I sniffed around, trying to locate where this lunch meat was, and this dude said, "Hey, girl. How about you help me make this go down?" I looked over and he had pulled his thing-thing out. It was over there twerking under the steering wheel. I'd found the meat.

I snorted. "Are you serious?"

That baloney smell was crawling up my nostrils and tickling my brain. I rolled down the window 'cause it stank so bad. The Wrangler had the kind of windows you wind down with a handle. I pulled a muscle in my elbow, cranking to let the smell out. He grinned at me and pulled the car over next to a parking meter.

"Yeah, I am serious." He leaned back in his seat, waving his D around, looking like he wanted someone to put a gold medal around it. "You're too beautiful. I need you to help me out."

"Okay," I said, "I'll help you out, all right." So I punched it.

More like slapped the hell out of it. *Whap! Whap!*

This dude cussed me out. "You crazy-ass bitch!" He was so mad, but I definitely made his dick go down.

"You should be ashamed of yourself," I told him. "You haven't even taken me to dinner yet."

Then we went to the Cheesecake Factory. When the waiter came to take our drink order, my thermos stayed in my bag. "I will take two vodka cranberries and a bottle of wine. And do you have any baby wipes for my friend over here?"

The Chinese chicken salad I ordered didn't smell too good, but at least it smelled better than his dick. When he took me home, I jumped out of the car and never saw him again.

Fellas, do not do that dumb shit.

I Like It Smedium

I prefer a smaller penis. I don't fuck with no micropeen, but four to six inches of meat is perfect. Smedium.

When they're big, men can be rude as hell, and they come and go when they want to. But men with just a few inches? Those guys are more respectful. They're kinder. They're more likely to be of service. They take out the trash. They rub your back. They snake your drain for you.

Listen, I'm lazy. If I didn't have to do it, you're gonna get it. If I come home and the dishes are done and put away and the house is vacuumed, you're gonna get your dick sucked. You clean out my gutters, get my oil changed, take my dog to the groomer? That is better than porn for me. You doing my chores gets me very slippery.

A smedium dude will leave my coochie panting. A dick that size is guaranteed to hit that good spot and make me squirm. Let's be honest. The average vaginal canal only goes about six inches deep. After that, you're busting that cervix and I don't need that kind of damage to my insides. It's too much. You're opening up things that shouldn't be open unless you're giving birth. If I get pummeled, I end up all swollen. Then the next day, I'm gapping because the swelling went down. A pussy will stretch and snap back to a point, but from my understanding, it's like a rubber band. If you overwork it, that thang will get loose. I don't want to have to pray over my vagina. I don't want to have to do tea tree oil and vinegar baths to try to bring her back together. So, if you have a big old dick, I'll pass. But if you have a little more than a few inches, get that thing over here and let me play with it.

Make Me Laugh

All of that other stuff is important for you to know, but the number one thing you have to do if you want to get with me is I want you to make me laugh. Women love men who make them laugh because laughter gets the juices flowing. I don't know about you, but when I laugh, my coochie flexes. It sucks together like I'm using it to pick up a marble. Ladies, go get a mirror, check it out. All those muscles contract when you laugh, so if you laugh during sex, it gets that D up there.

Not only that, but every single organ is getting massaged up and down when you laugh. It's like a cleanse, a detox. That's healing happening. I read a study about how crying and laughter are very similar in the way they wring you out inside, squeezing all the toxins out, but you use more muscles when you laugh than when you cry, so laughing is more healing,

You laugh because you have joy to spare, and it's spilling out your mouth. I'm looking for a man who is willing to share his joy with me. I gobble that shit up. Laughing during sex is a joy explosion popping off—like your soul is in a bubble bath of happy chemicals tingling all over.

When you are connecting and it's super primal, you're back to basics, just animals humping on each other—*uh, uh, uh.* All the shit—the stupid games, the worrying if you're good enough, the messy feelings—falls away and you see each other for real. If you let it, laughing during sex can be a totally unguarded moment (unguarded, not unprotected—I'm not trying to be somebody's baby mama), and you don't get a lot of those in life. You're connecting to something bigger than just a dick.

I want someone who can make Tiffnicity flex because my lady box? That's my root chakra right there. That's where creation comes from, where ideas come from. That spot activates energy through your stomach, through your chest, through your throat, through your mind, then you project your brilliance out into the universe.

So, if you want it, say something funny, motherfucker, I dare you.

I'ma Need Your Credit Score

Now, if you liked how I gave you the business, and you think you might want to come back around for more, maybe even date me, there are a few more things you need to know.

In my twenties, I was chasing, but now that I'm older, I know *I'm* the prize. To win me in a relationship kind of way, you've got to meet my criteria: fun to travel with, loyal, likes to dance, nice hands, physically fit, no kids, and willing to garden a little bit. You need to have your own career, like you've got things going on outside of me. I don't care what business you are in as long as you *have* business. I don't want you to focus on me 110 percent. I want to be number one, but I do not want to be so much a priority that you are psycho-crazy about it. I need some space in my life. You don't need to be like, "Oh, you going to the doctor? Let me get my phone. I'm gonna come with." I do not need you to come with me to get a Pap smear.

I want you to have your own universe where you can go get inspired and bring me back interesting things to talk about. I want you to be building a kingdom. I want to be with a king.

My favorite question to ask right off the top when I'm thinking about dating someone is, "What's your credit score?" That's your grown-up report card. Your credit score needs to be over 700. If your score is 700 to 850, that tells me that if you get a house and the gutters fall off, you can fix that shit. If you buy something on your Sears card, you'll be able to pay it off. When you retire, you're not going to be eating cat food. I'm responsible, and I need a responsible man.

Now if we are dating awhile and you start thinking about making things official between us, I could get down with that. But, if you want to spend your life with me, don't come at me with a ring. (I do not need a princess cut diamond from Tiffany's; I got all the Tiffany I need inside my own skin.) Come at me with some property. I don't want carats; I want *units*. Propose to me with an apartment building with both our names on the deed. I want you to get down on your knee and say, "Will you marry me?" and then open up an envelope with keys in it. *Then* I will say "yes." Maybe we get a ring afterward. We can get another nice place to live in together that's big enough that we won't be up in each other's business all the time. I want a man to make me feel good, but I don't want to feel your breath on my neck every time I use the fucking sink. We can make some brisket together and tell each other about our days—the big shit like what you're working on, but also the little shit like the time you saw a dog that looked like Richard Pryor.

And we'll cut each other some slack. You forget to buy the fresh coconuts I like to drink from? That's okay. You get a little soft around the belly? That's all right, too. If I don't like one of your posts on social media, no big deal. I want to spend the weekend with my girl-friends instead of going to your football game? You get it. The import-ant thing is there's you and me, and then there's the rest of the world. We're going to laugh together, support each other, and do awesome things for the community together because we're in a relationship. We relate to each other, and this ship is going somewhere. It's taking us somewhere *together.*

That sounds pretty good. Maybe we will get there someday. In the meantime, here's some markers. I'ma need you to color in this book.

DADDY ISSUES

GETTING THIS PHONE CALL had me fully fucked up. I wasn't sure what kind of man would be on the other end of the line or what would happen when we started talking. You see, my dad had not been in my life for almost two decades.

Twenty years. Long enough to go through two Vivian Bankses, three James Bonds, and four presidents. Last time I saw my father, Michael Jackson had just dropped *Thriller*. There was no such thing as the internet. *The Cosby Show* wasn't even on the air yet.

I didn't even have a lot of memories from the time I had had with my father to give me some idea of what to expect. I only remembered a handful of things—like him smoking cigarettes, how the smell came off him when I got close and stuck around in the air after he left the room. I remembered how one time he bought me a little Playskool typewriter to tap on and pretend to write stories about our family. I remember him taking me to Bob's Big Boy over in Culver City where he let me climb the Big Boy statue to try to get at that giant hamburger. There were a few other little things like that in my head, but the tape ran out pretty quick because my father disappeared—*poof*—before I turned four. He left my mama's house one day and didn't return. I learned later that my dad had been selling green cards illegally and he was worried my mom would turn him in to the police, so he'd taken off to keep from going to jail. But as a child, I didn't know any of that.

After he left, I looked all around for him, sniffing for his stale cigarette smell like a bloodhound, but he had fully peaced out. When I couldn't find him, I started asking my mama all the time, "Where's my dad at? Where did my daddy go?"

"I don't know. Shit. He's probably visiting his family in Eritrea. Now leave me be." You need to understand her man had just left; she had no patience for a little child asking her every five seconds where he'd gone off to.

I didn't have a clue what Eritrea was all about. Someone explained it was a small country on the east side of Africa, but that didn't help much. Closest thing I could picture was a messed-up image I'd gotten from those old commercials about how you could help a starving child in Africa with a big belly and flies all over him. That's where I imagined my dad—far away in Africa, surrounded by family, people he obviously loved more than he loved me.

For years, I played "Are you my daddy?" with every man who walked down the street. If the back of your head looked like his, I thought maybe you were my daddy. Garbage dudes, the school principal, the bus driver—they all got my hopes up at one time or another, but it was never him. I started looking for my father for real when I was sixteen. I'd thumbed through every phone book I could get my hands on, trying to find his name in there. I guess I wasn't looking in the right places because I never found him. I came to the conclusion that I was the only Haddish left in all of America.

I spent my whole childhood jealous as hell of girls who had fathers. Dads who put them up on their shoulders at block parties so they could look out over the crowds and feel ten feet tall. Dads who made sure they returned with the correct change when they sent them to the corner store. Dads who gave them a look that said, "You'd best be tying a flannel around your waist before you leave my house," when they wore booty shorts.

No matter where I looked, it seemed like everyone had a dad but me. Around a third of families in the US are headed by single moms, but popular culture doesn't give us a lot of stories of girls with no dads around. There are plenty of full-on orphans in children's stories. But if a princess loses a parent in a fairy tale, it's usually her mom, not her dad. Where was the story about being raised by a single mom? *Murphy Brown*? A rich white woman with a confusing relationship with her contractor didn't exactly speak to my experience growing up in South Central Los Angeles. Now, if I had had a single dad, there would have been plenty for me to watch: *Diff'rent Strokes, My Three Sons, Punky Brewster, Full House, Blossom*. Hell, it was easier to find TV shows about aliens living among us than shows about girls with no dads.

Even most of my friends had dads who'd stuck around. I couldn't believe how blind they were to the everyday joy of having a dad. They didn't know the pain of living without one. In high school, I'd be hanging out at a friend's house after track practice while her dad watched TV in the living room. She'd go in to ask him to drive us to the mall and if he said no, she'd sass her father. I'd think, *How could you talk to your dad like that? At least you have one. He's showing up. He's walking in the door every day. He's putting food in the refrigerator. Yeah, he might be getting on your nerves, but you've got a whole family. You're complete.*

When I was a teenager, I had a job as an "energy producer" at bar mitzvahs. I'd watch as girls would do the father/daughter dance. Their dads held them as they glided around the party to "Beautiful Tonight," and I would just cry on the inside. Or sometimes, if I was on my period, I would fuckin' cry on the outside, 'cause why didn't I get that? Why didn't I have a father who loved me and held me like that? What was so wrong with me that I hadn't been enough to get him to stay?

A lot of single moms, when they end up with no man to help them with their kids, their love expands like gas in a room, just getting bigger to fill the empty space. When my mom's head crashed through that windshield, it was like it broke her love valve. I was always trying to suck those last bits out of the air to keep me going. She was not interested in loving me anymore—and she wasn't interested in what I had to give either. She'd take one look at my love and be like, "Wrong address, return to sender." I used to think maybe there'd been some kind of mistake. How could I love this woman so much and she didn't love me? I hoped I'd been switched at birth and that maybe there was another mom out there waiting to fill me up with love. It made me want to run away to Africa to find my daddy and get away from my mama so I never had to deal with her again. I thought I'd go to Africa and they'd accept me into their tribe like some *Color Purple* shit. I'd get some cuts on my cheeks and then I'd have a whole village of people that loved me. Like I said, I didn't have the most informed view of Africa at the time. I just knew anything had to be better than getting beat on. I staggered around for twenty years hungry for the kind of love I saw all around me. I covered it up pretty good, but that empty spot in my heart echoed with longing.

Which brings me back to this phone call. It happened when I was twenty-seven years old. I'd finally managed to get a message to my father that I wanted to speak to him.

I was in my shitty little one-bedroom apartment. I had been rehearsing lines for an audition by the futon in my living room when the phone rang in the kitchen.

"Hello?" a voice said.

My heart pounded. *Dadumpdadumpdadumpdadump.* There I was, a grown woman, connected for the first time in forever to my daddy by satellites across the miles and years.

You know how in *Jerry Maguire*, Renée Zellweger's character tells Tom Cruise, "You had me at 'hello'"? My father had me at "hello."

It was the wildest trip to hear that voice. Directors have said to me, "Tiffany, we can never find anyone to dub your voice. There's no mistaking Tiffany Haddish. It's like your voice has this special code in it that no one else can produce." When I heard my father speak, whatever special code was in there activated something in my spirit that made me feel whole. It was pure animal instinct, like a dog bum-rushing its owner when they come home from work.

I used to think if I ever reconnected with my dad, I was going to go over and kick him in the dick so hard he'd never have any more kids. That way he'd never be able to abandon anybody else and leave them feeling like they weren't worth shit. But now that I was actually on the line with him, the last thing in the world I wanted was to kick him in the balls. I wanted to bury my face in this man's side and fall asleep in his arms. If he'd been in my life, I wouldn't have thought twice about a phone call from him. I might not have even picked up a call in the middle of the day like that. But because of all I'd missed out on, I now wanted to hear every single word he had to say. I wanted to know every single goddamn thought he'd ever had.

I sucked in a little breath. "This is Tiffany Haddish." There was a pause and then he said, "My daughter."

"Hello" had made my head spin, but "My daughter"? Ohmigod. I was like a little baby, reaching out her hands, grabbing like, "Please, please, pick me up, Dad. Please, please, please. Hold me, hold me, hold me."

My spirit lifted, and my eyes started filling up with tears. A few of those tears ran down my face and fell onto some marijuana plants I had growing on my kitchen windowsill.

Then he said, "You sound so grown up." That brought me back down to earth real quick.

"Well, you know, I *am* grown up. It's been a long time since we last spoke. I'm twenty-seven years old." I'd spent thousands of hours picturing this man in a thousand different places—in Africa with his people, in Israel with his fellow Jews, in a phone booth about to put a quarter in the slot to call me and then changing his mind at the last second—but I'd never really known where he was. Now I could finally ask. "Where have you been, Dad?"

His words rushed out. "I've been all over America. I've been everywhere. I've been in Vegas. I've been in Dallas, Texas. I've been in Florida. Right now, I'm in Philadelphia, but I'm going to Virginia." He paused to take a breath. "Tell me, Tiffany, how many grandchildren do I have?"

He really did not know one damn thing about me. "You don't have any. Not from me."

I could tell he was disappointed to hear that, so I started asking him eighty thousand million questions. As he answered, I leaned way back and pushed my chin up to keep the tears from running in my mouth. We talked for over an hour. He had had a whole life without me. I told him all about my life without him—about my mom's accident, about how she'd gone to a mental institution, about my brothers and sisters and how we had been in foster care. I told him everything.

I could hear him gasping. "Ah. But your mother, she was so beautiful, so smart." I told him that she was still beautiful and that she was still smart in there somewhere, but she was also damaged.

"You had a house. Does your mom still have the house?"

There was a little hope in his voice that maybe not everything had gone bad, but I had to tell him. "No, she lost the house. She lost everything." It was quiet for a minute. I pictured him closing his eyes on the other end of the line.

He asked about my grandma and my aunties. When I let him know that one of my aunties had passed, he said, "Oh, your auntie, such a fighter. So strong. Such a strong spirit. How did she die?" I had to tell him, "She got shot in the back."

Every fact I shared with him was another layer in the guilt sandwich.

We both stopped talking for a minute. It was quiet, but the silence on the line was as loud as a thunderstorm. Then he said, "I'm so sorry for not being there."

You might think that's exactly what I wanted to hear. But the thing was I didn't want him to feel guilty. I wanted our reunion to be a jubilee, a celebration of this big moment in my life. *I had a dad again!* I had been angry for so long, but now all I wanted was to make this man proud of me.

He told me he wanted to see me as soon as possible. He said he wanted to know everything about me. We had so much lost time to find, so much to learn about each other. One phone call was just the start.

After we said goodbye, I hung up and thought, *I'm going to show him that even though he wasn't there for me, his DNA did a good thing. He did something amazing. Even though he didn't nurture me or raise me, I came out really good.*

A few weeks later, I went to Virginia to meet my dad in person for the first time since I was a kid. I didn't know what would happen when I got there, who this person would be. I did hope he wasn't as ugly as my mama said he was.

He'd been living at his girlfriend's house in Richmond. I got out of the car, and when I first saw him, I went, *Whoa.* I was glad I knew he was my father, my flesh and blood, because had I met him in a bar at a dark comedy club, he could have pulled me. Dude was very handsome. We looked kind of alike, me and my dad. We were about the same color, but he was a little shorter than me and had short curly hair.

"Tiffany, is that you?" Again, that accent went straight to my soul. "Yeah, it's me."

We stepped forward at the same time and reached out for a hug. As we held each other, I could feel his heart beating in his chest. The same blood ran through our veins. This man. *My father.*

He smelled just how I remembered. I inhaled real deep. After a minute, I pulled back, still holding on to his arms with my hands, and looked him over. He had the same little fingernails I have. I'd always wondered why my fingers were shaped the way they are. Nobody on my mama's side of my family had them. Turns out, they're my daddy's fingers. He invited me inside and as we walked I noticed the way my foot goes to the side, his foot went to the side, too, when he walked. I couldn't take my eyes off him. The more we talked, the more I noticed so many things we did the same, body movements that mirrored each other. We chewed the same. When I sit and relax, I kind of slump up a bit. He did that, too. And we both liked wearing windbreakers.

I could tell he was trying not to cry. Man, that made two of us. He told me everything about Eritrea and about joining the navy, about coming to the States and meeting my mother. He showed me pictures of himself and his family. He showed me a photograph of his mother and told me that where she lived in Eritrea everyone knew her. She owned a spice business, a bar, and a lot of land. Apparently, she was very funny and personable, but in this photo, she had serious eyes and braids tight on her skull. My father told me what he remembered of his dad, who had died when my father was like five or six.

I didn't ever want to leave him. I wanted him to get in the car with me right then and there and move in with me in California. But I didn't say that out loud. Instead, when it was time to go, we promised each other we would stay in touch—and we did, calling each other at least once a week to check in. Now that I had my dad back in my life, I wasn't about to let him go.

A couple months after I first spoke to him, my dad gave me away at my wedding. That day was supposed to be a celebration of the life I was making with my new husband, but what I remember best about that night was how my dad and I danced together during the reception. He placed his right hand on my shoulder and his left held mine as the DJ played Luther Vandross. We circled the floor while I cried like an ugly fucking animal. I finally had my father-daughter dance.

I wish that was the end of this story—a happy ending with me dancing like a princess at the ball—but it's not.

For the next several years, my dad and I talked regularly on the phone. I'd call him up and tell him how my gigs were going (pretty good), how my relationships were going (pretty bad), and what my plans for the future were.

My dad became a sounding board for me and my problems. Anytime I had an argument with a boyfriend or I was having trouble communicating in a relationship, I'd call my dad to ask, "How do I talk to this man?" He tried to counsel me and told me he'd be there for me if I needed him.

When I left a long-term relationship, I called my dad and he comforted me.

"This is a chance for me to protect you. I'm going to try to get me a place, a two-bedroom apartment, and you can just come stay with me. Just come stay with me." He made me feel like I would always have a home with him.

In 2008, my father moved from Virginia to California to go back to college. Not a four-year college but more of a career school. The following year, I went to his graduation. He was so excited to show me off to all his classmates, leading me around and introducing me to everyone as his daughter. One of them said, "Oh, I saw you on *Who's Got Jokes?*—you're so funny."

My dad's face lit up with pride. It made my heart swell up to have someone claim me like that. I had spent every damn moment of my life as a kid trying to get that approval from my mother, to get her to smile at me and go, "That's my girl."

When I got back home from my dad's graduation, I decided I was gonna show my mom what her baby could do. At the time, she was still living in a mental institution, so I drove over there to show her the video of me on *Who's Got Jokes?* Maybe she'd be as proud as my dad. She'd see me perform and be like, "Yo, all that mean stuff I said to you for all those years? I was wrong. You are amazing. I'm so proud of you, Tiffany. I love you."

In the rec room at her institution, I shimmied my shoulders a little as I slid the tape in the VCR. A bunch of the other residents pulled their folding chairs in a semicircle around the TV on its metal cart to watch my set. The tape whirred and the static gave way to a grainy image of me doing stand-up for the judges. Pretty soon, those folding chairs were squeaking against the floor because the residents were laughing so hard, their big "ha ha has" shooting across the room like a meteor shower.

As soon as the video was over, my mom stood up like she was queen of the galaxy. She looked at me, then she looked around at everybody in the room as if she was gonna make an important announcement. *Hear ye, hear ye.* I stood there with my chest out thinking, *This is it. My mama going to tell all these people that I did good and she's proud of me. Okay. I'm ready, Mom. Go ahead.*

She lifted up her chin and said to the whole room, "My pussy makes stars!"

The fuck?

She didn't say, "My baby girl did so good!" Or "Isn't my Tiffany so smart, so talented?" No. She said, "Look at what I did. I carried that in me. Had it inside for nine months, spit it out, fed it. It survived, didn't die. Now, it's on fire. It's a star. I did that." It was about the most narcissistic thing a person could say.

The average human, if they heard their mom say that, would be like, "Bitch, you crazy. Your fruit loop had nothing to do with it." But I'd take what I could get. I felt like she saw me, like she recognized that I was trying to do work that meant something. I could have retreated like a wounded animal and cut my mama out of my life, but I'd already lost my dad. I knew how much that sucked. I wasn't about to lose her, too. I had to dig for the good in that moment, but I found the joy.

Even now, there will be times when I wake up at 2:00 a.m. so I can make a 3:00 a.m. call time after not having had a day off in seven months—so tired that I want to go to sleep and never wake up—and I'll wonder, *Am I doing all this, working myself to the bone, just for my mom's approval?* You know what? Kinda. Yeah. We all just want to be seen and appreciated, especially by the people we love.

In 2012, my dad came out to see me do a play in San Francisco called *What My Husband Doesn't Know.* After the play let out and I had changed into my street clothes again, I found my father outside. He said something to me I didn't quite catch—something about how he needed to teach me magic—but I was just so happy to have my dad in the audience after all those years, I didn't ask him what he meant. He was always promising to teach me things, like Tigrinya, the language of Eritrea. "I must teach you the language of our people." He never got around to it. He never did get that two-bedroom apartment either, but he was there on the other end of the phone when I needed him. I was always very grateful, very loving, which just seemed to confuse him.

He would say to me, "All of my friends, they were in their daughters' lives, and those girls are so mean to them. I am so blessed. Why are you so nice to me?"

I thought about my high school friends and how they'd taken their fathers for granted. I wasn't about that. After all those years without him, just being able to talk to him on the phone meant everything.

For the most part, I *was* nice to him—except when I had had a few drinks and drunk-dialed him. Then I let some of the anger out. There may have been some cussing.

The first time I called him drunk, I said everything I had wanted to say during the time we were apart. I let him know how fucking sad and alone it made me feel. How broken.

"You weren't there for me, Dad. Bad shit was happening in my life, and you were not there for it."

I wasn't sorry I'd said it, but I knew it had to hurt to hear.

Then he said something I'd wanted to hear my whole life: "Tiffany, you are always right to me. You never, ever can do anything wrong. If nobody in the world thinks you're right, I'll always think you're right."

You remember in *Cinderella* when they're putting the gown on her over her head and the air around her starts twinkling and there's a magical transformation? It was like that for my soul. When I performed, people would come up to me and go, "Oh, you are so funny! We love you, Tiffany." And I appreciated it, really, but was I missing the whole world's love? No. I was missing my family's love. My mom's love. My father's love.

When my father said that I was always right in his eyes, it had nothing to do with what I had done or what I had accomplished.

This wasn't just a matter of him being proud. He was saying he loved me no matter what I did—not because I had sold out a show, not because I had made a bunch of money (which I hadn't yet—I was still broke as hell at that point), and not because it was his sperm that made me. It was just because I was Tiffany. It was like I'd been held underwater for most of my life, my lungs screaming, "Bitch, you better get some air in here or you about to drown!" until finally, my dad pulled me up to the surface. I sucked in all the oxygen the atmosphere had to give me. I drank it down, gulping, greedy for it because that shit is what makes you fully alive. I wished I would have heard someone tell me I was worthy of love years ago when I was a little girl. But when my daddy said it, it was right on time.

I wish *that* could be the happy ending of this story. I finally heard the thing I most needed to hear my whole life, but that's not the ending I got either.

In 2016, my dad came out to visit me in LA. In the middle of our visit, he had to go to the hospital. By then, he was in his sixties—an older man who had smoked for years and his heart had had it. I went to see him. He wouldn't tell me shit about what was going on.

None of the staff would tell me what was going on either. I heard him tell the doctor, "Do not resuscitate." I said, "What? No, we resuscitate. Definitely resuscitate."

He was there for a couple of days while I worried my ass off about him.

When my dad was ready to be discharged, I picked him up, got his medications from the pharmacy, and tried to get him to tell me what was going on with him. He was stubborn and refused to say anything specific.

He was back up on his feet a few weeks later. I thought he was steady enough that I invited him to my gumbo party for the first day of the new year. I was feeling festive. I had all these people—friends, neighbors, family—over to my house, drinking and laughing and having a good time. My dad didn't look totally comfortable. Was he noticing the life—the career, the friends, the home—I had built without him? I have no way of knowing, but he ate a little gumbo while folks played cards at the coffee table. I leaned against the doorway taking it all in. It was the first time I could remember sharing the new year with my dad.

For a few hours, the party was humming. Food on every plate, drink in every hand, smile on every face. I took a minute to appreciate a sense of satisfaction with my life. My career was going well—I was on *The Carmichael Show* and had a big role in *Keanu*. I had a house, a good group of friends to celebrate with. My fucking dad was there. Not bad, Haddish.

I went outside in the backyard to check on the kids jumping in the jumper when it hit me that I hadn't seen my father in a while. I scanned the yard for him, but no luck. I went to the room he was staying in, and he wasn't there. I looked in the whole house, which didn't take long 'cause it wasn't that big. "Where's my dad at?" I asked, but nobody knew. I kept asking around until someone finally told me, "Oh, your dad walked out the door like two hours ago. I think he went to the store or something."

I started lighting up the cell I had given him for Christmas. For the next few hours, I was calling him, calling him, calling him. No answer. Before I knew it, it was one o'clock in the morning, and I was getting worried. Two in the morning, he still wasn't answering.

My boyfriend at the time said, "Maybe your dad got a girlfriend. Maybe your dad went to go see his friends. Who knows. He a grown-ass man. Stop worrying."

But I couldn't stop. I didn't know where the fuck my dad was. Rewind the tape. I was that little kid again, tugging at my mama asking, "Where'd my daddy go?" Somewhere inside me, though, I knew he was already long gone.

Then, finally, at eleven o'clock the next morning, while I was pouring half-empty cups down the sink, my dad called me to say he had gone home to Chico.

He hadn't even said goodbye.

We fought about it. He told me he didn't feel like a good man and that he wasn't a good dad. He didn't deserve to be with me or around me and that he had let me down. He had failed me.

"No, you didn't, Dad!"

I tried to say back to him all the things he said to me that had made me feel like I was in a fairy tale where dreams come true. "But you were only right. You were only right. You gave me life, Dad, and I turned out to have a *good* life. Maybe if you had been here, if you had been around to raise me, I would have come out bad. Maybe I would have come out not funny, not loving. So maybe I wasn't supposed to be raised by you . . ."

But he didn't listen to that. He said, "No, it hurts too much. I'm not a good enough man. I don't deserve a daughter like you." And then he hung up.

It fucked me up.

When he had walked out of my life the first time, I had nothing to do with that. That was on my mama and his crimes. Nothing to do with me. But the second time he walked out, it was about his ego. It was about him, but it felt like it was about me not being enough. I was right back to feeling like I was alone in the universe with no one to protect me from shattering into a billion pieces.

I called my father every single day after that, even though he didn't answer. Over and over, I dialed his number and left a message, but he never picked up, never called back. Then my calls started getting to once a week. I kept doing little things for him. I sent food, paid the light bill for him, called him on his birthday and sang "Happy Birthday" on his voice mail. That last time, my voice must have worked its DNA magic because later that week he called me back.

"Okay," he said, "you can come see me in March. Come to my house."

My heart danced a little in my chest. I was going to get my daddy back again.

I set up everything so I could go and see him. I called a few days later to give him the details and he stopped me. "I don't know if you should stay at my house. Maybe you should get a hotel."

I thought he was nervous or embarrassed for me to see his house. "Dad, I'm coming. I don't care what your house look like. I don't give a damn if you got seven hundred roaches. I'm getting ready to come." He didn't say yes, but he didn't say no, so I made up my mind to go.

The day before I was supposed to leave, he went off on me on the phone. He screamed at me at the top of his lungs. "I don't want to see you! I don't want you to see me! I don't want you here! I don't want you to see me like this! I'm not good enough!"

He screamed to keep me away from him. He felt so much shame that he didn't even want to be seen.

I felt myself slipping beneath the surface of the water again, pressure building up in my lungs. "But I love you, Dad."

If I'd never had him back in my life, I would never have known how light it felt to walk through the world with my dad by my side. I'd been cursed with the joy of knowing my dad. I knew exactly who I'd be missing. That's why I was so breathless. The loss was already heavy on my chest.

"I don't believe you. All my friends tell me that you lie to me, that there's no way you can love me because I didn't raise you."

I was reaching out to him through the phone, trying to grab him with my words. "Your friends don't know me. They don't know my heart. And, Dad, if you believe them, frankly, you don't know my heart either."

Looking back, I think he knew he didn't have much time left and was taking stock of his life. The shelves were emptier than he would have liked. I think the guilt of not being there, of not being the man that he was raised to be, not having the fortune he had before he came to America, not having all the things he wanted to have, not being a part of my life, not having the family that he grew up with, that ate him up. Maybe there had been something about seeing me in the life I had and knowing I had built it all by myself without his help that was too much for him.

I was shaking, but I told him, "I will honor you. If you don't want to see me right now, okay."

I never saw him again.

We still spoke on the phone and FaceTimed a little bit, but there were no more visits. Eventually, the phone calls petered out, and I stopped hearing from him entirely. I was heartbroken.

In May of 2017, I was in Vegas filming when I got a call. It was a weirdly cold night for Vegas in the spring, and I shivered when I answered.

It was a nurse from the hospital in Chico calling to tell me that my dad was dying.

I tried to make my voice sound normal as I thanked her and asked her to please hand my father the phone. She came back on the line and said he didn't have that much energy, but he had used the strength he had to push the phone away. I asked her to put the phone up to his ear and tried to think of what I could say that would give him something to live for. I knew my father had always wanted me to have a baby, so I tried yelling, "Daddy, I'm pregnant. I'm going to have a child!" But those words just evaporated into space.

Before long, he was no longer responsive. The nurse told me if I wanted to come say goodbye, now was the time, but I was determined to honor my father's wishes because I would want someone to honor mine if I was about to leave this earth. So I stayed put.

Two days later, he was dead. He's been gone for almost seven years now.

You know what's crazy? I still call the phone I gave him that Christmas and leave voice mail messages that are like the conversations we used to have—or my half anyway.

"Daddy, I miss you. A lot of good things are happening for me. I'm pretty happy with who I am most days. I wish you could be here to see it. Why you don't call me back?" Then I play it back, and I hurry up and delete that shit.

He left for good this time. He won't be in the audience when I perform ever again. There won't be any more calls where he reassures me. No more stories about his family. I remember one call we'd had, after he had gotten out of the hospital in LA, where he brought up the magic he'd mentioned after he'd seen my play in San Francisco. He promised he was going to teach me some magic. Some people would call what he was talking about witchcraft, but it's really our roots, our tradition.

"With this magic, no matter where you go, you always will have help. You always will have somebody to help you. When I see you again, I'm going to teach you."

I pictured us getting some sage, some frankincense, and buying one of those little charcoal burner things like what they roast the coffee beans on to burn the herbs. I imagined my dad would say some words in Tigrinya for me to repeat. Then this big puff of smoke would come and cover me. After we did this spell, everyone I met would be mesmerized and would feel love for me. That sounded good to me.

I kept bugging him about it, but he kept putting me off, so I let it go. The thing is, he *did* teach me. He *did* give me that magic.

By loving me unconditionally even when he couldn't love himself that way. Not for what I could do for him. Not for the money I made or even the jokes I wrote. Just for being me. That was some real witchcraft. For a time, he had given me that missing piece. He showed me what it was like to feel whole. As much as it hurt to lose him, learning to love the child inside me who was always going, "Pick me up, hold me, love me," was better than anything. Like my girl Whitney Houston said, it's the greatest love of all.

I miss you, Daddy. I hope you know you were always right to me.

MY INHERITANCE
A BIG ASS AND AN F'ED-UP
VIEW OF RELATIONSHIPS

I BELIEVE THAT GOD gave each of us three brains. We have the brain in our head, the brain in our heart, and the brain in our gut. All three of them weigh in on the decisions we make. I can tell when I'm making a good choice because all three of my brains are lined up. My head brain can't come up with a reason it's a bad idea, my heart pounds with joy at the prospect of doing it, and my gut is like, *Yeaaaaaah, we gotta do this*. When my three brains are singing the same tune, that's God coming through in harmony. But if the sound any of those brains is making is a little off, that's the devil doing his dirt, whipping up some discord and shenanigans. Basically, if it feels off, I shouldn't do it. Any doubt, do without. That's damn good advice—not that I always listen to it.

I don't usually talk about this part of my life, probably because I'm embarrassed I got played the way I did. Nobody likes to think of themselves as a punk, but there was this guy, Reginald, who I fooled around with on and off for many years beginning in my twenties. Dude broke my fucking heart.

I met him at a bowling alley in the early 2000s. I was with my friend Chrissy when Reginald and his homeboy walked in the door. My first thought was, *This dude is trouble. No question in my mind that he is absolutely no good . . . but, man, he sure does* look *good*. He had on a shirt that was so tight you could tell he had a lot going on underneath. Not like he spent all his time at the gym but still cut. I like a little pooch in the belly on a man, like he's got to doo-doo or something, but the abs are still there—a coochie bumper, I like to call it.

I turned to Chrissy. "I bet you I could get those two fine-ass dudes to come bowl with us."

She sucked her teeth at me. "Bullshit."

I don't lose bets, so I rolled up to Reginald full of swagger, pushed my hip out, and said, "I love your FUBU shirt. That's dope. [Big smile.] You should come over and bowl with us."

And they did. *Pay up, Chrissy.* We had a good time bowling. I made sure to bend way over every time it was my turn to bowl to show off dat ass. At the end of the night, Reginald wrote his number on an M&M wrapper for me, and we were off to the races.

This dude really had me going, especially once I saw him with his clothes off. I have always liked a man who, if shit went down and we needed to run, could pick me up and carry me to safety—or at least to the end of the block. Reginald was so big, my ear only reached as high as his chest. Whenever I hugged him, I could hear him swallow. His whole upper body was ripped as hell. He was a barber, so maybe it was from holding his arms up all day cutting hair. I don't know.

He didn't take me out much, but I would go over to his mama's house in Hawthorne. He had a place in the back; they'd turned the garage into a dwelling of sorts. We would talk and laugh and smoke weed and fuck. We had such a good time with each other. It was very natural. We didn't just bullshit like I did with a lot of the other men

I'd dated; we talked about all sorts of things—emotional things, philosophical things, spiritual things. "How much do you think the soul weighs?" and "Do you believe in past lives?" Man, we would talk for hours. Sometimes, we played these brain games that are supposed to keep your mind firing and active. There was one to boost your vocabulary called Verbal Advantage. Another improved your memory. We pushed each other intellectually. He was always asking me to try to make my comedy smarter. He wasn't mean about it. He just had high expectations of me.

"Yo, why you doing that wack shit? You are smarter than that." That relationship was edifying. (That's a word I learned from Verbal Advantage.) He gave me edification and good penetration.

I felt like he was seeing all of me, not just my vagina, you know? That was a great feeling. I used to look at him across the room and think, *I could fall asleep on this man's chest. I could sit in his lap, and he could burp me like a baby.* That sounded real nice because once you become an adult, nobody does that for you. No one picks you up, rocks you to make you feel safe, and goes, "Come here, baby. It's okay, it's okay. Everything is going to be okay."

I really saw myself in some fantasies with this dude. I thought me and Reginald were going to be the Black Cleavers—nice house, a family, two-car garage, good jobs, barbeques on weekends. We'd have inside jokes that we'd laugh at together. We'd have a bunch of kids and take them on vacations, sleeping in a camper curled up together like a litter of puppies. We would take pictures of our beautiful family in front of different monuments and then hang the photos up on the walls to remind us how lucky we were. I'd never had that kind of picture on the walls of my house when I was a kid. My mom and dad, they loved each other at one point, I think, but it wasn't exactly a picture-perfect situation.

My mom met my dad at a gas station when she was twenty-one. He'd recently come to the United States from Eritrea as a refugee when the country was at war. He was very handsome with a soft Afro and a smile that made other people want to smile back at him. My mom thought he was the bomb. She made it her mission to help him adjust to life in America. She taught him how to drive because cars were not that common in Eritrea at the time, so he'd never learned. She taught him how to speak English and how to get around, basically making his entry as smooth as possible. My dad must have been pretty smooth, too, 'cause my mom started sneaking off to have sex with him whenever she could. Within six months of meeting him, she was pregnant with me.

Thing was, my mom was Jehovah's Witness, and the Witnesses don't approve of sex before marriage. Hold on to your drawers because this next bit is fucked. Instead of confessing she had been sleeping with my dad, my mom told the elders in the congregation she had been raped and that is how she got pregnant.

Even though I was very small when my parents were hiding their relationship, I knew something was off. They didn't do what other parents did—like live in the same house together, make breakfast together, or take me to the playground together.

When I got older, my dad loved to tell me about how I would come into my mama's room in the morning to wake him up. I'd put my warm little kid hand on his shoulder and shake him and say, "Daddy, Daddy, get up! You're not supposed to be in my mama's house. I'm going to tell my grandma next time I see her because you're not supposed to be in my mama's bed until you marry my mama."

I don't know who ratted my mom out to the elders. It might have been one of my aunties who snitched or maybe one of my mom's friends, but they eventually found out she was in an relationship with my dad.

Not that it mattered for long because he left a few short years later. After my dad left us, my mother was so fucking pissed off she even told *me* that he had raped her. She dropped that on me one day when

I was around seven. She had gotten together with my stepdad by then and had a couple of kids with him, too. My stepdad looked like Al B. Sure—tall, skinny, and light-skinned with good hair that naturally curled up, so it looked like a Jheri curl. I guess he was good-looking for the eighties. But he and my mama fought like they were two rats who'd found one chicken bone. They were always yelling at each other. Big, nasty fights that seemed to make cracks in the walls and let evil spirits into our home.

She and my stepdad were in the middle of a throw-down where they were shouting at each other so loud it made *my* vocal cords vibrate. I couldn't stand the yelling anymore. I turned to my mom and asked, "What are you even doing with this guy? You guys argue all the time. Just go back and get my dad." She slowly turned away from my stepdad and slapped me with the back of her arm, then pushed me away.

"You miss your daddy, huh?" Satan's fire flashed in her eyes. "Well, your dad used to beat me, and he raped me. You wouldn't even be here if he didn't rape me."

That knocked me on my ass quicker than any shove.

Da fuck did she say? My daddy *raped* her? That didn't make sense. I knew they hadn't had the best relationship, but if what she'd said was true, why had he been around all the time when I was younger? Who lets their rapist sleep in the house with them? Who goes out to a steak dinner and goes dancing with them? My young brain couldn't make sense of it. It was like a math puzzle with no answer in the back. I believed her for a long time. I mean, there were seeds of doubt.

After all, her brain wasn't totally right from the accident, and my aunties were telling me that my mom had really loved my dad, but it wasn't until I reconnected with my father in my twenties that I stopped thinking I was the product of rape. He might not have raped my mama, but he did leave her.

It says in the Torah and the Bible, you inherit the sins of your father. Well, my inheritance from my parents was a big ole ass and a fucked-up view of relationships. No point in letting anybody get really close; they're just going to leave anyway.

You know when you're hungry but you don't have the thing your body needs—green vegetables or a nice brisket—so you eat ten pounds of whatever you have around the house instead—Doritos or Red Vines or whatever? You ate, but you're still empty, still hungry for something that will nourish you? That's how I felt about having someone show me what it would be like to be in a good relationship. The models I had gave me a bellyache, but they were all I had to put in the tank. Then, in high school, I met Ted and Kimberly.

Ted and Kimberly were my friends' adopted parents. They were very big Christians, churchgoers. They're the most amazing white couple of all time as far as I'm concerned. They adopted my friend Dimante when he was ten, and then they adopted Nick when he was fourteen. Nick and Dimante were both Black. Nick was my boyfriend for six months in high school when I was a junior. I called him "Nick, Nick with the big old dick." He took me on my very first real date. We went to the movies and Kimberly drove us, like something out of that show *The Wonder Years*.

Nick's family welcomed me into their house after that first date. Ted and Kimberly were what you would call involved parents, and that included going to all of Dimante's football games and being involved with both their kids' friends. They weren't nosy, they just asked questions that showed they cared. Walking into their house was like walking into a hug. I was living with my grandmother at the time, which was a whole other scene compared to their big freaking house with its swimming pool. I broke up with Nick a few months later, but I still hung out over there all the time—not just because of the pool but because I liked being around Ted and Kimberly so much.

I'd seen couples around who seemed happy together. Not every relationship in South Central was an episode of *Cops*, but you never know what goes on behind closed doors. The man who looked like Husband of the Year at a holiday party might be a nasty mother-fucker at the dinner table. Ted and Kimberly's house was my first close-up look at a couple in the privacy of their home when they weren't on their public behavior.

Ted and Kimberly were like my best auntie and uncle. Ted was a lawyer and consultant. Kimberly was a doctor who ran a healthcare organization, which was impressive, but what I liked about her best was how she really believed in me. She came to my plays and sat cross-legged, leaning forward in her chair where my mother would have sat if she hadn't been in an institution. I remember one night after a drama competition (which I won, thank you very much), all the actors were chopping it up. Kimberly pulled me aside. She touched my shoulder with the tips of her fingers and told me, "Tiffany, the way that you control a whole auditorium of people, you know you're magical, right?"

I felt like a cat soaking up the sun. For a kid who wanted nothing more than to hear praise from her own mother, that was a shot of happiness right to the heart. That's the key to developing as a healthy human being—having other human beings believe in you. Like Snuffleupagus. Or the Velveteen Rabbit. Having someone who says, "I think you can do it. I think you are awesome." That right there is enough to kick you to the next level and the next level. Ted and Kimberly did that for me, for their kids—and for each other.

You could tell they were each other's number one fan. They really respected one another. When they argued, they never yelled at each other or threatened to set each other's hair on fire. Their fights were super civil conversations. I got to hear them disagree when they picked me up on the weekends to go to church in Long Beach with them. If they disagreed about directions, it never escalated beyond, "You don't have to say it that way. There are better ways to communicate." If Kimberly lingered to speak with her friends after services, Ted would put his hand on her lower back and move her toward the door. As we drove home, she'd say, "I don't know why you were rushing me off from my conversation." Not "Who do you think you are? You don't own me. I'ma slap your controlling ass into next week." And almost every disagreement they had ended with a little kiss.

Then they'd go off giggling at each other like they'd never disagreed in the first place.

Who fought like that? Why wasn't anybody yelling? Where was the name-calling?

When we got back to their place, Nick and Dimante would grab Cokes from the fridge and say, "Come on, Tiffany, let's go to the TV room and listen to *Ready to Die*," and I'd be like, "You go ahead. I'm going to sit here and listen to your parents argue a little longer."

I'd watch Ted smiling at Kimberly and I'd think, *That's the kind of husband I'm going to have when I grow up.*

"Husband" has always been my favorite word. It represents something steady, something you can count on. I go out of my way to say it as much as possible. When my friends started getting married, I would call them up just so I could be like, "What's your *husband* up to, girl? Oh, you with your *husband* taking the kids camping? Is that your *husband* I hear in the background?" Eventually, they were like, "Why you always asking about my damn husband? You trying to fuck him?"

I wasn't trying to fuck anyone else's husband. I was trying to have my own husband. I didn't need the whole wedding—the dress, the cake, the party favors of candied almonds wrapped in lace. I just wanted to be able to say, "Let me talk to *my husband* and find out what *my husband* wants to do." 'Cause we would be a team, my husband and me, working shit out together like Ted and Kimberly.

When I met Reginald, I thought he might be my husband.

Whenever he would come over, I would try to act like we were a serious couple. I'd fluff up the pillows on the sofa, dim the lights, and cook for him like we were playing house. He'd wrap me in those big fucking arms, and I would feel so safe. At last, I thought I had what I wanted. A man to hold me and make me feel loved. A partner.

I slept at his house four nights out of the week, but he never invited me out with his friends. Never made plans with me more than a couple hours in advance. Dude couldn't be bothered to take me out for egg rolls. I should have known these were signs he wasn't respecting me. The brain in my gut kept piping up, "What's up with that?" But I just ignored the queasy feeling I got anytime he refused to come out with me and my girls or when he canceled plans at the last minute.

Then one night after we'd been hanging out for two years, I dressed up nice and went over to his mama's house. We were kicking it on the couch he got at Big Lots, smoking some weed and listening to some music. I felt all soft and snuggly. I sank into him and felt trust crack open in my heart. *This man is going to be my husband.*

I looked up at Reginald and thought, *I want to do for this man. I want to do for him for the rest of my life.* I was sick of having a boyfriend. That boyfriend shit was for the birds. Chicken-heads to be exact. I was a grown-ass woman; it was time I had a husband.

I started to tell him about my vision of our life together, of what we could be—the two of us linked up for the long haul. I was really getting started with some ideas for our future when I heard, "Why don't you shut up and just suck my dick?"

Excuse me? I was trying to tell him I saw a life with him and he wanted me to shut my mouth? Around his dick? That little crack of trust closed up real quick, like someone had slammed a door in my heart.

"What you say? You can't talk to me like that."

He rolled his eyes. "Bitch, just suck my dick. Shit."

If someone were to say that to me now, it would be a full situation. Treat me good, I'll treat you good. Fuck with me, and I'll stab you in the heart. But that night, as soon as the words were out of his mouth, my brain in my heart was already putting a spin on it. "Okay, yes, that was disrespectful, but you're going to spend your life with this man. He's probably having a bad day. Why don't you leave, let him chill out, and come back another time? He'll make it up to you."

I grabbed my purse and peaced out. I went home and cried all night. And then cried more the next day, and the next. I was crushed. Why did Reginald not see us together the way I did? Had he just put me in the ho bag category? But what about the way we had pushed each other intellectually? What about all the times we had felt so good and relaxed together? What was wrong with me that he didn't see me as the total package?

Months went by and Reginald did not call. Not once. I guess I had hurt his feelings when I walked out of there like that and he was letting me know by icing me out. I should have closed that chapter and moved on.

But, the whole time I was crying, the brain in my gut was telling me, "He's going to come back around. Just you wait. He's going to and when he does, it's going to be a main thing."

Props to my gut brain because it was right. He did come back.

It was like nine months later when we reconnected. My dog had just had a whole litter of pit bulls I was selling. I got a call from Reginald saying, "Hey, can I check out your dogs? My dog died. I need another one." Enough time had passed that I wasn't thinking about him much anymore. But the minute I heard his voice, my vagina was yelling at me, "Go get that dick. I miss that penetration!"

He came by to look at the dogs. We stood outside with the puppies licking on each other next to our feet. I tried to keep my eyes on the dogs so I wouldn't look at him. Every time I did, my inner ho was like, "Bring on the dick!" He picked out a dog, and we worked out a trade where he would cut my brother's hair in exchange for the puppy, which meant I started seeing him and his big, beautiful arms on the regular. The brain in my head was like, "You sure you want to be doing this? You know this dude has not changed one bit. If he was not interested in you as a person before, why do you think he'll suddenly be interested in you now? Why are you thinking about him so much again? Go read a book or something. Get some edification." But my heart and my gut were shouting, "Shut up, head brain. That man hits it so good and makes us feel so safe and happy." It was two against one. Next thing you know, Reginald and I were back to fucking.

This time around, we were even more domestic, always at each other's places, having dinner and talking like we were an old married couple. He would come over to my place and he was cooking *for me*. He got the spaghetti bubbling on the stove and some cookies on a fancy plate, and we'd watch *Dexter* together. I started to think that I'd been right all along: What I had with Reginald was going to be something real. Mind you, we still didn't go anywhere in public as a couple. I wasn't thinking about that, though. I was just thinking about how much fun we had and how real it felt when we were together.

I could see us raising kids together someday, being all up in their lives like Ted and Kimberly were with Nick and Dimante, but not invasive. We'd be the cool parents, the house where all the kids in the neighborhood would always feel welcome. Our kids would never have to wonder if they were going to come home to a cage fight or whether one of us was going to ride off into the sunrise never to be seen again.

That part of our relationship lasted for about two years. Then, one night after some chicken and dumplings, Reginald and I were making out over at his place. It was very romantic with Maxwell playing in the background, and Reginald started fucking me without a condom. I didn't freak out or kick him out of the bed. Not at all. Opposite, in fact. I thought, *Oh yeah! This is happening. He must want me to have his kids because he's trusting me with his sperm. He really loves me.* I was as happy as could be.

A few days later, I was still riding that happy feeling when Reginald called me at two o'clock in the afternoon. "Guess what, girl? I got a brand-new vehicle. We are going to San Diego. Get your things. I'm going to pick you up in an hour."

I went into my bedroom immediately and started packing my bag, thinking maybe I should pack some extra lotion for my hands so they'd be soft in case he busted out an engagement ring.

I was ready by 2:45 p.m., sitting at my window, watching the cars go by, wondering what his new car was going to look like. Hours passed and passed with no sign of Reginald. Five o'clock came around, he still hadn't showed up. Six, seven, eight, nine o'clock came and went. Every fucking car in LA drove by my house that day except his. He was not answering any of my phone calls. I moved my overnight bag back into my bedroom. My head brain started to go, "I told you so," but I didn't want to hear it. I crawled under my covers and sucked my thumb until I fell asleep.

The next day, I tried to call Reginald for the twenty-thousandth time, but his phone had been disconnected. So, I called my friend who worked at the phone company and figured out how to pay Reginald's phone bill. He was going to be my husband after all. By the next day, the phone was working so I called again, but he didn't answer. I got my homegirl to call. He answered but then hung up on her right away.

Can you believe I still couldn't see the reality of the situation?

I made excuse after excuse. Maybe he went to buy me a ring and some boys stuck him up and now he was being held hostage, but he couldn't make a run for it because he was going to be a father to our child soon and running would be too dangerous. Maybe he wasn't used to his new vehicle and he got in a car accident and was in a coma and thought his name was Marcellus Wallace. Maybe one of those sinkholes opened up on La Brea and swallowed him and now he was neck deep in a tar pit. I sat in my house for *three fucking days*, waiting for him to show up.

Finally, I called his mama's house to ask where he was at. His mama said, "Oh, Reginald? He went to San Diego with his girlfriend for the weekend."

Girlfriend? I thought *I* was his fucking girlfriend.

I'd been messing with this dude on and off for *years*. I let him fuck me without a condom because I thought that meant he loved me. That's a lesson: Just because he doesn't want to use a condom doesn't mean he love you. Here's another: Just because he cooks a meal for you does not mean he cares about you. Also: Just 'cause you sleep in his bed four nights out of the week does not mean anything other than you are a belly warmer. Someone else might be there the other three nights. Those were some hard fucking lessons to learn as a young woman.

After finding all this out, I was ready to ruin somebody's life. I was definitely mad at Reginald, but—you saw this coming, right?—I was also mad at myself. How could I have let myself get worked like that? I had wanted that good relationship, that dream family like Ted and Kimberly had, so intensely that I bent the truth in front of me to make my life fit into a dream.

It was like I had put one of those drawings architects do when they're going to renovate your house over a photo of how I was really living. It looked the same if you squinted, but if you lifted up the drawing, you could see rats had eaten the foundation and it could fall down and crush somebody any second. But I wanted that house to protect me *so bad*, I ignored how wobbly things were. At that point, the only thing keeping me standing was my rage. It came up through my ovaries and came out my eyeballs like a supervillain's.

I got so fucking mad that even the devil got scared. I was never going to be Reginald's wife. This was not my man. This was just a dumb motherfucker who was toying with me. He didn't really care about me. Good thing I hadn't gotten pregnant by him because if he'd had a baby with me, he would probably treat that baby badly, too. I'm lucky I found out when I did. The fantasies I started having then were very different from the white wedding / Black babies fantasies I used to have. I'm talking Timberland boots to the nuts, hot bricks to his face. I was going to sneak over and give him some Ambien. *Nighty night*. And then, while he was asleep, I was going to bend a paper clip into my name, heat it up, and burn "Tiffany" on his dick. I'd put mud and salt on it so it would keloid over and be ribbed for pleasure. When he woke up, I was going to look him dead in his eyes and tell him to his face to keep my name out of other bitches' mouths.

I thought about that. Oh, I thought about that a lot. But I didn't need police to show up at my house and lock me up over this motherfucker. So, here's what I did instead.

Reginald had left a few things at my apartment—T-shirts, basketball shorts, socks. He'd left me hanging right around Father's Day, so I put all his stuff in a box and wrapped it up in Father's Day wrapping paper that had little ties all over it. I got him a Father's Day card and wrote inside, "It was amazing knowing you. You're a really interesting human being. I learned so much from you, and I know you're going to be a great father to this baby." Then I took the box to the barbershop he worked at and put it where all his coworkers could see it. Didn't hear from him after that.

You know what's really fucked up though? For years afterward, I still thought about that dude. I knew I needed to let him go, but I would fantasize about going over to his house and sitting on his dick every once in a while. Worse than that, I still get a little pang in my heart when I think of him. I even have that M&M wrapper with his number on it stored in a box with some photos of him.

The human desire to couple up with someone who loves you is so strong. It's written in our genes. To find that good love, some of us have to fight through some messed-up ideas of what relationships look like. Maybe if I'd grown up with parents who had a relationship more like Ted and Kimberly's, there wouldn't be so much fucking static jamming the communication between my three brains and I'd be able to see right away when some fool isn't worth my time or energy. I'll admit, there are times I worry I'll never find someone to love me the way Ted and Kimberly love each other. It sucks when I have no one to go home to but my cat and my dog. They are sweet and all, and they love me unconditionally (or the dog does anyway—that cat got her own thing going), but you can only feel so much connection with a creature who licks its own ass. When it's quiet and I can hear my mind, my heart, and my gut speaking together as one, they remind me, "Watch what you say to yourself, girl. The lies that hurt us most are the ones we tell ourselves." I've got to remember to listen to that so I can get out there and find a man who is worthy of this beautiful ass.

CAN I GET A WITNESS?

I SPENT A LOT of my childhood at the Kingdom Hall of the Jehovah's Witness. "Hall" is a pretty good description of the building we went to every week for services. It was a low building, not a lot of windows, so no matter what floor you were on, it was like a basement. You go into a Catholic church, and it's like, "Check out all this stained glass! They got all kinda polished wood in here. Is that real gold? Damn, this is like the Queen's house." The Jehovah's Witness Kingdom Hall had more of a convention center vibe, like a place where you might go for a workshop on how to invest in real estate. But because the Hall wasn't fancy, you felt welcome there, like you didn't need to worry that you might accidentally break God's good dishes.

The Jehovah's Witnesses were perfect for me early in my life because they gave me a community I could lean on when things were falling apart at home. They fed me, clothed me, and looked out for me in a way my family couldn't necessarily.

One of my favorite parts of going to the Kingdom Hall was singing with the Witnesses. There was no choir. Nobody was a trained singer, but every person in there held their songbooks open in front of them like they were offering them up to God. Whether they knew the melody or not, they'd sing—good voices, bad voices, didn't matter. They all equaled out when they joined together singing Jehovah's praises. It was the most beautiful sound in the world. I'd turn around and see all the joyful people around me and go, "Look how many brothers and sisters I could have," because once you're baptized into the Witnesses, they call you Brother this or Sister that, like you all belong to the same family.

I'll bet you a hundred dollars you have ducked your ass down on your dusty floor when you saw the Jehovah's Witnesses coming to your door. "Turn the TV off, Janelle. Close the blinds. Hurry up!"— as if you were hiding from the FBI. Like the worst thing you could imagine was a very polite lady with some pamphlets about Jehovah interfering with *Jeopardy!* She was just trying to share God's truth with you, maybe hand you some literature. What were you so worked up about?

It takes a lot of guts to go up to a door knowing it will probably get slammed in your face, and the Jehovah's Witnesses know that. That's why they make sure you're prepared when you go out to do your field service. (Field service is when you hit the streets to spread the Word.) They don't just hand you a stack of *Watchtower*s and slap you on the back—"Good luck out there. Don't talk to any strangers— unless it's about Jehovah!"—they build up your skills so that you don't get discouraged. One of the ways they build you up is by having you do these sketches to teach you how to approach people and get them to speak to you. You role-play different scenarios to encourage people to read the Bible more—maybe even get them interested in what it means to be a Jehovah's Witness—so you can bring them into the family.

My first performance must have been when I was around seven years old, before my mom had her accident. Sister Williams, who I thought was the bomb because she always had a butterscotch candy or a peppermint in her purse for me, invited me to do a skit with her. It might surprise you to learn I could be very shy as a little girl, but I was. Despite my shyness, I was excited to be asked to get up onstage because I loved to act out stories. I would always try to copy different characters from the shows I was watching on TV. I started wearing a cowboy vest with tassels on it after I watched *Bonanza*. I'd pretend to be on *Little House on the Prairie*, running around in a bonnet that tied around the neck. That must have been hilarious—a little Black girl in prairie clothes tearing through the neighborhood going, "Call me Laura Ingalls!"

I could tell my mom and grandma were pleased I'd been chosen to be in the skit with Sister Williams. It was like a stamp of approval from the church. The Jehovah's Witness Kingdom Hall was my mother's favorite place to be. That was where she'd go after a week of running herself ragged at the post office, doing demos in the grocery store, and looking after kids. We went to all the services. She was very involved in church activities, planning parties for the teenagers and doing Bible studies. Once a month, she'd take me to a get-together the Witnesses threw in the Kingdom Hall. I loved those get-togethers. The whole community was there, playing cards or some kind of board game, and there'd be food to share. The people attending might not have been your friends if you had met them anywhere else, but because you were part of the Kingdom Hall together, you got along. It was like a family reunion every month.

Every once in a while, somebody hosted a get-together in a back-yard. You'd see the married couples two-stepping and doing the cha-cha while the elders looked on from the patio. The elders stepped in if we kids got to squabbling, sending us off to separate corners to cool off because Witnesses looked out for one another.

If I were a single parent, I would definitely join a Kingdom Hall. Morally, the Witnesses are on it. They make sure all the young ones come correct. I like what they stand for—informing each other, sharing God's Word, sharing knowledge. Every Kingdom Hall has a library. Ours was in the back of the Hall where the new moms would sit with their babies so their fussin' didn't interrupt services. That's where my family sat, too—in the back, where no one could stare at us because our clothes were not the best.

Witnesses are also extremely practical. After services, they send you over to meet with the elders to learn how to deal with certain issues: how to be a more productive parent, how to be godlier in the workplace, how to maintain a good relationship with your spouse—a bunch of different how-tos for your soul, but also really down-to-earth how-tos. They gave instruction on gardening, making clothing, working with your hands, and the art of taking care of the home. All these different life skills every week. I give them a lot of credit for that and for making young ones get up and perform in front of everyone.

When it was my turn to do that skit, I wanted to slay. Problem was, I knew it would be my job to read a little Bible scripture up onstage and I couldn't read that good, even compared to other seven-year-olds. I could recognize the shapes of the letters, so I could show you where all the books in the Bible were, and I knew the order of Genesis, Exodus, Deuteronomy, and so on. So, if somebody said, "Turn to Corinthians," I knew it started with a C and where that was in the Bible, so I could just flip, *fft, ffft, fft,* Corinthians. *Ta-dow.* But could I read the actual words of the scripture? No.

I felt a lot of pressure to do a good job. What if I got up there and made a fool of myself in front of all my Brothers and Sisters, and they decided I was the black sheep of the family? Actually, we were all Black sheep. Not a lot of white people in the Kingdom Hall in South Central Los Angeles in the 1980s. I just didn't want to get a reputation as the stupid Witness. For all of their good qualities and quality programming, Witnesses had a lot of rules to follow and not a lot of wiggle room. You weren't allowed to have a beard if you were a man or wear tight pants or short skirts to the Hall if you were a woman. If you went on a date, it couldn't be just the two of you. You had to have a chaperone along. Kids weren't allowed to join groups outside the church like the Boy Scouts, although that one probably saved a lot of little Witnesses from getting their willies touched, so maybe they were smart to have that rule.

I made a plan so I wouldn't embarrass myself in front of the whole congregation. I got Sister Williams to read the Bible passage for our skit to me over and over until I had it locked in. Back then, I was a memory champion. If someone read something to me a couple of times, it sank deep into my brain tissue where I could fish it out whenever I needed. Memorizing was my superpower. My power weakened after I learned to read as a young adult because I didn't need to rely on my memory as much anymore, but when I was younger, I was the Michael Jordan of memorizing.

The day of the performance, I had on my good shoes and a church dress I had gotten as a hand-me-down from one of the other members of the Kingdom Hall. It was brown-, turquoise-, and green-striped with flowers in the stripes. There was a lace collar and a lace panel with some bootleg mother-of-pearl buttons in the front, and it tied in the back. I had on stockings because I loved pantyhose. I felt so cute, like my outfit was worthy of my big moment.

I walked with Sister Williams to our marks and smiled like we had rehearsed as the whole Kingdom Hall watched and waited for me to begin. I wasn't old enough to have stink in my sweat yet, which was good, because I was nervous as a mofo.

I'm going to stop you here and tell you something: If you dig in and do some research, you will find out some of the best comics—the most hilarious and successful comedians—grew up with Witnesses. Mike Epps, Katt Williams, the Wayanses—Witness, Witness,

Witness. I think it's partially because growing up Jehovah's Witness is boot camp for getting an audience to pay attention to you. That's your job as a comedian, figuring out how to get strangers to listen to your journey. Witnesses teach you about charisma, how to smile through awkwardness, how to read other people's signals, and, of course, how to handle getting shut down. It takes thick-ass skin to be a comedian. When you're up onstage, you're offering a little bit of yourself and hoping other people accept your offering. It can be scary as hell to put something out there and not know if it will be welcomed or rejected. Learning how to go door-to-door was good practice for doing a set. If you can interrupt people at home when they're going about their business or as they are walking down the sidewalk to get to work, ain't no thang to get up in front of a room full of strangers who paid good money for you to entertain them. Plus, they're probably drunk anyhow.

Up onstage at the Kingdom Hall, I thumbed through my Bible. I had it marked where to turn to, so I opened it up like butterfly wings and started reciting:

> The one who examines me is Jehovah. Therefore, do not judge anything before the due time, until the Lord comes. He will bring the secret things of darkness to light and make known the intentions of the hearts, and then each one will receive his praise from God.

I held the book so it looked like I was reading, but I wasn't. I was double-performing. When I glanced up from the pages into the crowd, I was selling it. My mom and grandma looked up at me from their seats and started clapping. Pretty soon, everybody was clapping because it was my first time doing a talk for the congregation. If it's your first time, everybody claps. I felt like I had passed a test, even if I had cheated.

Afterward, I mingled with the audience, basking in the feeling of being let into a club I'd always wanted to join. I was feeling all warm and happy among my Brothers and Sisters when the girl whose mama gave me the dress came up to me and laughed right in my face. "Check you out in my old dress, Miss Tiffany. You don't even look cute in it. You look all skinny and scrawny."

There went the warm and happy. I twisted my face up, trying not to cry. It was like she saw straight through me, and it sucked the sense of belonging right out of me. That was cold.

The Kingdom Hall was where my formal religious education started, but my mama was the center of my spiritual universe. My sun. She talked about religious stuff all the time when I was little. She'd be making hot dogs in the kitchen and she'd talk to me about Jehovah this and Jehovah that; Jesus Christ is not God, but He is Jehovah's son; and Jesus is coming back, and Jesus is going to heal us. That was food for the soul. One day, as I was setting the table, she started talking about how Jesus died to save us from our sins. That got me paying attention. "Why would He die for people He don't even know? That's confusing."

She tucked napkins under the plates and explained how we were all God's children, which meant we were part of God's family, like Jesus. He was like our brother. I thought about that a minute. In my short life, I had seen plenty of bad behavior by God's children, and Jesus had been dead a long time. Shit, I had just tricked the whole Kingdom Hall into thinking I could read. If God had died to clear all of our sins, it hadn't worked.

"Okay, so if He died for our sins, why are we still sinning, then?"

She breathed out hard like she didn't have time for my smart ass. "Well, then He just died for those people's sins at the time when He lived. He cleared their sins, but then we still got to live in sin."

"So, I have other people's sins on me?"

That's when my mom dropped an analogy. She said if you're baking bread in a baking pan, and if you bang it and it has a dent in it, then every loaf of bread you make in that pan is going to have a dent in it. No matter how hard you try to knock the dent out, it's still always going to be a little bit messed up. It's never going to be that perfect pan that it was before. And every time you bake something, it might get a little worse, a little more dented in, a little more crooked, a little more lopsided. That's how it is with our sin. We inherit our mother's and father's sins. The only one that can fix it—truly fix it and take all the dents out and smooth it—is the expert at making those pans. That's God. God is the baker and He don't feel like fixing no damn pans. That's what my mama said. At least, I *think* that's what she said. Mind you, I was seven, so I could be off about this.

I did some God math in my head. If God was the only one who could fix us, He must also be the only one who could say if we needed to be fixed—the only one who could judge us. But that was confusing to me, too, because there were a lot of times where I felt so much judgment from my fellow Jehovah's Witnesses. *If God is the only one who can judge me, why does it feel like there's so much judgment here from these people on earth?*

My relationship to the Kingdom Hall changed after my mom's accident when I was eight. For the first month, while she was in the hospital recovering, I lived with my great-grandmother in Colten. This was in the '80s when three-way calling started to get popular, so the Kingdom Hall let us dial in and listen to the service on speakerphone with another family. Then when my mom came home, my grandmother would take the whole family twice a month to the Kingdom Hall and occasionally to Bible studies at someone's home. My mom loved to come because it was familiar to her. She might not have recognized people by name or known who they were to her, but there was still something comforting about being around them. It got her mind going, brought back memories. Plus, it was good for her to be around adults. After a year or so, though, I stopped wanting to go to the Hall. Because my mom wasn't functioning on all cylinders, it fell on me to get my brothers and sisters ready every week. I did my sisters' hair, got my brothers dressed, tried to make sure we were on time. But I could feel people judging us when we showed up, even if we were in the back of the Hall. We didn't have the best clothes. We weren't the cleanest. My little brother, Lance, was running around in pissy clothes. I would lay out the clean clothes for him, but he kept his pee-pee clothes on. I could feel other people's eyes on us when we walked in, and it was like I could hear what they were saying in their heads: "What do those kids got on? Who is taking care of them?" I took that as a personal insult. Even though I was doing my best, I was not a mother. I was a child. Having other people, including adults, judging me, that was a lot.

By the time I was eleven, I started flat-out refusing to go to the Kingdom Hall. I was tired of feeling like I was being shunned by other members of the congregation. My mom didn't want to hear about me feeling judged. She'd whup my ass until I got in the car.

Then, from ages thirteen to fourteen, I didn't go to the Hall because I was in foster care. Those families weren't trying to drive to worship somewhere outside of their faith. It wasn't until my grandma got custody of us when I was fourteen that I started getting with the Witnesses again. It's not that I suddenly wanted to go to the Kingdom Hall, but I wanted to get away from my mom when she came over to Grandma's house on Sundays.

My mom would show up at my grandma's house ready to *fight*. It was either go to the Hall or stay home and fight with my mom, and I didn't need anyone calling the police on our house.

I went to the Kingdom Hall just to escape. I'd sit with my grandmother, hiding out from my mama. I didn't necessarily feel like a member of the congregation. I felt like a fugitive, like I'd been turned out by my own family.

After a while, I started noticing other people in that hall who were hiding in plain sight, too. People who were there but not there. They came to the Hall, but no one acknowledged their presence because they had been disfellowshipped. That's when you get officially kicked out of the Jehovah's Witnesses. I saw people get disfellowshipped for a mess of offenses—drinking too much, cussing too much, having sex outside of marriage, getting divorced, spreading rumors, or telling lies on people in the Kingdom Hall.

When you get disfellowshipped, you're basically canceled from the congregation. No one talks to you. No one is allowed to associate with you. You are totally cut off. You can keep coming to the Kingdom Hall, but nobody will sit next to you unless they absolutely have to because there's no other seats. You're the smelly kid at school. Your friends never call you. They don't say "hi" when you're walking down the street. People look right through you like you're a ghost. Imagine going up to your best friend who you had just talked to the week before, saying, "Hey, girl, what you doing?" and she just looks past you like you aren't even there. That'll make you question your whole existence. The silent treatment is some coldhearted business. Therapists actually qualify it as emotional abuse. Loneliness can kill you, same as smoking or drinking or eating so many Snickers you give yourself the sugars. We humans are pack animals. We need each other to survive.

What killed me about watching these people who were ostracized was knowing my mama had gotten disfellowshipped when I was a baby because she had gotten pregnant with me out of wedlock. On the list of sins that could get you kicked out of the Witnesses, that was more or less right up there with murder. I had known that she'd been disfellowshipped, but I hadn't fully understood what it meant until I got older and watched it happen to other people. Once I saw how you got treated, I saw how super painful it must have been for her to lose her place in the Hall. 'Cause, like I said, that place was her life.

My grandma had told me how Mom had worked really hard to get reinstated into the Jehovah's Witnesses. She had to go through some extra Bible study to prove to the congregation that she really did want to reenter the community. Took her six months, but she'd gotten back in the game.

I watched the Sisters and Brothers at the Kingdom Hall look right through people, reach past them to get the potato salad, and let doors close behind them like they were nothing. It did look a lot like abuse. Because of the way my mom acted toward me, I knew what it felt like to not belong in your own family.

In the classes after services, I'd been learning about how when you get baptized, it is a contract between you and God—between you and Jehovah—to do your best, be your best, love Him, honor Him. But if it was a contract between us and God, how was it that humans were going to determine that someone doesn't get to be in the congregation anymore? Didn't you just tell me it's God who gets to say who is right? Then how come it was a bunch of humans who were icing out people like my mom who had been disfellowshipped? How come they were the ones making me feel ashamed of my shabby-ass clothes and of the job I was doing trying to be a mother to these little kids?

I owe the Witnesses a lot. But there came a time in my life where I had to say goodbye and thank you to the Witnesses because I found a different set of windowless rooms where I felt like I belonged.

Over the next ten years, starting when I went to the Laugh Factory Comedy Camp, I spent more time in comedy clubs than I did in the Kingdom Hall. There was a camaraderie with comics that reminded me of the feeling I used to get at the Witnesses' monthly get-togethers as a kid. Comics looked out for one another, too. I noticed they would hug each other all the time, even after a bad set. I didn't get that many hugs coming up, so to get that felt really good. Plus, it felt like comics knew when to withhold judgment. You could eat a bag of dicks onstage, and another comic will come up and pull you in because you were brave enough to get up there and express yourself. Nobody pushed you aside over one bad night. Of course, there are assholes like in any other business, but most comedians will always say "good set, man." They cut you some slack because they know how hard it is to be vulnerable up there.

You know how they say there's the family you're born with and the family you make? The Jehovah's Witnesses were like the family I was born with. But the comedy world, that's the family I have made. The Laugh Factory became like a home to me. That was where the family gathered. The comedians there took time to nurture me, help me grow. They encouraged me to look at the who, what, when, where, why of my life to find the jokes. I'd hang there with Bill Dawes, who was like a brother to me. When I was living out of a car held together with duct tape and coat hangers, he didn't make me feel like shit that I was homeless. He offered to let me stay in his apartment for free.

There was also Lil Rel Howery and Cory Fernandez, who I met when we were doing *Who's Got Jokes?* I liked their act so much, I walked up to them afterward and said, "You two are going to be my friends. Give me your phone numbers." And they did. We'd have forty-five-minute conversations where we laughed so easily it felt like we were born together.

Finesse Mitchell used to give me dating advice, telling me not to be so aggressive with men because when I'd go up to a guy all, "What that dick do?" it was making them think I had herpes.

Then there was Chris Spencer. He has always looked out for me, even before I was famous. Whenever I was going through some shit, he'd call to check up on me. He took me under his wing, taught me the fundamentals of booking shows, helped me get my start.

I got a sister early on, too. Aida Rodriguez. We started out talking about where the best comedy rooms were and what it was like being a woman in the business, but then we became close. If she'd had a late show and didn't get home until 1:00 a.m., I used to talk to her on the phone in the early morning hours to keep her awake while she drove her kids to school.

What really did it for me and the Witnesses was their take on comedy. They didn't fully accept me the way my fellow comics did. When I was doing Bible study with them during a difficult period in my life, two elders and one of their wives had a talk with me. They didn't explicitly forbid me from going out onstage to perform, but they made it very clear they did not approve of my style of comedy. They thought I should be like Sinbad and make jokes about shoes, not about my unmentionables. You're not supposed to be a worldly enter-tainer if you're a Jehovah's Witness. You're supposed to be humble and modest. You are definitely not supposed to be cussing in public. I could do a clean show, a PG-13 show, but it didn't feel natural. To me, that's like having sex through a sheet. Yeah, you're doing it, but it's not much fun.

But listen, I have read the Bible a gang of times. Let me tell you, that is one of the freakiest books ever written. I have found references to milk, honey, breasts, spilling seed, cheating spouses, wife-swapping—some of the passages are very sexual, especially in Psalms—but nowhere in there did I find a part that said, "No telling jokes."

I couldn't believe that God didn't want me up onstage spreading joy. That was the straw that broke this comedian's back. You cut me off from comedy, you cut off my oxygen supply. I don't know how I could function without it.

So, I kept doing stand-up comedy and said farewell to the Witnesses. What's funny is that some of those Jehovah's Witnesses from my Kingdom Hall would come to my shows, and they'd be in the audience laughing as hard as anyone else.

I'm not about judgment because when you judge people, you're assuming you are better than someone else. Those people in the Kingdom Hall looking down their noses at my family's clothes, they didn't have the right to judge us. And I don't have the right to judge anyone else because I don't know their whole circumstance. I'm going to give them the benefit of the doubt. I don't think I'm better than anyone else. It's not my job to pee for anybody, and it's not my job to tell them how to go about their business here on earth. That's between them and God. If you make a mistake in your life, I'm not going to disfellowship you. If you wrong me, I put it in God's hands—so do not lie to me if you don't want gum disease because I am one of His favorites and He listens to me.

Human judgment means nothing unless I'm in court. No one can cancel me but God. That'll be the day I leave this planet. I'll tell you what. I'm going to live my life my way until He comes knocking at my door.

SHARK WEEK

LET ME ASK YOU something. Have you ever seen a Black actress on Shark Week before? The answer is no, you have not, because Black women have enough bullshit to deal with. We do not need to be jumping into a feeding frenzy to get our blood flowing. But here goes the thing: I had always had in my mind that a dream vacation—just the most relaxing thing in the world—would be to dive off the side of a fancy yacht into sparkling blue water. I wanted to sit in a lounge chair on a polished deck, let the sun get me good and roasty under a bright blue sky, and then leap off the edge and let that cool water wash my stress away. I had been on cruises, and I had jumped into a lot of swimming pools, but I had never dove off a boat into the sparkly ocean. So, when I got a call from discovery+ asking if I would be willing to do Shark Week on location in the Bahamas, I was into it.

Now I'm missing a leg.

I'm just playing. But for real, don't fuck with sharks.

Let me tell you some things I found out about these creatures when I did a little research. They can have *fifty* rows of teeth in their jaws, and they go through more than thirty thousand teeth in a life-time. Sharks can smell a single drop of blood in an Olympic-size pool because two-thirds of a shark's brain is dedicated to smell. If you are cut and bleeding, if there's even a little blood pouring out of your body, I would suggest you do not get in the water with sharks. These fools don't even have bones; they are all muscle, gristle, and cartilage, so you can't break them. Even their skin is made up of thousands of little razor teeth that can mess you up if you rub it the wrong direc-tion. All of that had me thinking twice about accepting the offer, but on the other hand, the image of that yacht was calling me, so I agreed to be part of Shark Week. I figured if I died, worst-case scenario, my family was going to own a TV network.

The trip started out well. They set me up in one of those hotel rooms where everything is white: white chairs, white comforter, white desk, white walls, even the white guests were whitey white. At sunset, I sat in a white chair watching these little yellow-bellied birds dance around my windowsill.

I settled in, had a couple of drinks, and then fell into my fluffy white bed and floated to La La Land, dreaming about that ocean plunge. The next morning, I woke up to the sound of palm leaves rustling outside my window. I took my time to get myself looking *foine*. A sleek blond wig, an orange one-piece suit cut high up the thigh, white sunglasses, strappy blue heels, a floppy hat, and I was ready for my day on the water. I had to hold on to my hat in the ocean breeze when I arrived at the waterfront to begin filming. A little salt got on my lips. Boats kissed the pier with little lapping noises, and my heels sank into its soft gray wood as I strutted down the dock like it was Fashion Week, thinking, *I am about this yacht life.*

That feeling did not last long. Y'all, this boat they put me on was not a luxury yacht; it was a *science boat.*

There was no champagne, no waiters, no little sushis being passed around on plates—none of that. All this boat had was a whole lot of equipment—cameras and ultrasounds and measuring tools—and bowls and bowls of shiny fish guts covered with flies. You had to pee in a bucket, and everything stank.

I stepped on board and got my balance while the ocean rocked the boat like a big cradle. The shark specialists clomped on with even more equipment in backpacks and bags that thumped against their legs. I was introduced to a very nice white lady scientist in a navy blue polo shirt. I noticed she had one of those Dramamine tabs behind her ear. She smiled at me as she held on to the side of the boat, but from how white her knuckles were on that railing and how stiff her knees were, I got the feeling she was thinking, "How long 'til this is going to be over and I can get back in the lab?" Like she was the kind of scientist who was happiest looking at data, not swimming with sharks.

The captain took us out far into the ocean but not so far out where you couldn't see land. I think the cameras made my girl even more nervous because she kept grabbing at my arm the whole ride. I got up in her grill and asked her a bunch of questions. *What kind of sharks are we going to see? How big are they? What do they eat? What eats them? Can you make a purse out of a shark? Why not?*

When the captain cut the motor, you could hear seagulls yelling at the boat, *Gimme some of that chum.* But the specialists were saving that for the sharks. Once we got settled and the gasoline smell cleared from the air, they started tossing globs of it into the water.

That was when things got real. I looked over the side of the boat, and there was already a bunch of sharks gathered beside us. These were some big-ass sharks. Nobody had told me before I got to Freeport that the Bahamas are known as "the shark capital of the world." They also hadn't told me that, back in 2003, one of the shark specialists got bit during filming. I wasn't scared, exactly, but my heart rate definitely sped up when I saw the size of these sharks. "Ten feet long" might not sound so big when you read it on the internet, but in real life, where I was close enough to get splashed when they jumped out of the water, a ten-foot shark looked as big as a Dodge Ram, only with a thousand monster teeth snapping.

I am not someone who *likes* to get scared. I don't go out in search of thrills and chills for the adrenaline rush—except for once a year during Halloween I'll go to a haunted house. Back in 2019, Ellen DeGeneres sent me through the *Us* haunted house at Universal Studios with her producer, Andy, for her Halloween show. I wore my leather moto jacket like I thought I was hard, but before we put even a single toe inside the haunted house, my brain was acting like a Black woman talking to the screen at a scary movie. *You better watch out, Tiffany. Lupita clone gonna get you. You're gonna come out of there with a bloody shirt. Or wet jeans.* Andy had barely gotten a hand through the curtain before one of those red jumpsuit dudes from the movie leaped out. *What the fuck?* I took off running like I was Flo Jo herself. After a minute, I calmed myself down and worked up the courage to go inside. We walked around the first corner super slow, but that was a mistake because the slower we went, the more time it gave my imagination to go buck wild. Anticipation is the worst because the human mind is so creative it can make up things a billion times scarier than what the world puts in front of us. I started breathing heavy, sounding like I was about to come. *Heh, heh, heh.* But then when I screamed, it was not "Yessssss!" It was "Ahhhhhhhwww! Ahhhhhhhwww!"

As we made our way around the twists and turns, Andy kept saying I needed to look out for decoys, for ways my brain was tricking me into being afraid of things that were not actually going to come for me, but I was like, "No, that's not a decoy. That's real! That's real!" And I was fucking right. Every damn thing in there jumped at us. But that haunted house was designed to take advantage of the way our minds spin out to get us hollering. In real life, a lot of what we are afraid of is not real. We fuck ourselves over, imagining every goddamn way things could go wrong. Like they say, fear is false information appearing real. You can't let false information make your choices for you.

That first day of Shark Week, the schedule called for us to free dive, as in no cage. There would be nothing but a centimeter of rubber suit between me and these sharks. I knew I would be safe—the producers didn't need a lawsuit on their hands, so they weren't about to put me in a situation where I could actually get hurt—but I did get a little lightheaded because one of my biggest fears is being eaten alive. You try and name something scarier than a lion holding you down with paws as big as your head while he slices open your throat. You're weaker than he is, and that motherfucker knows it. He's like, "Oh, you tryna take my picture and scare off all the antelope? I will eat the skin right off your face." That wouldn't even kill you right away. You'd still be alert as he was gnawing at your neck like you were a turkey leg. *Grrrr num num num.* There is no more terrible way to die. So, yeah, getting eaten alive is something I definitely didn't want to happen to me.

But then, because I'm a scientist (and proud graduate of YouTube University), I know that we're actually getting eaten alive every day. There's something eating off you *right now.* You have yeastie-beasties on your skin at this very moment that are eating up all your dead skin cells. You might have fleas in your house, or you might go for a walk and get bitten by mosquitoes or ticks. You've got parasites inside your intestines chewing up your food. For the most part, it's nothing to be afraid of, which is good because you can't go around being afraid all the time.

Fear is like an app on your phone you can't delete. The manufacturer installed it, and you can't get rid of it no matter how many times you drag the icon to the trash can. You know it's bullshit, but for some reason, you can't get it off your fucking phone. You can try to delete it, but it pops back up with the cloud arrow icon pointing down, downloading nonsense into your system—God gave us fear for a reason—but it's not the only tool. If you rely on it too much, it will drain your battery, making you too afraid or too exhausted to try out something new. It will make you avoid risk, which is death for a comedian.

When I was doing comedy in my early twenties, I didn't have the swagger I needed to kill every night. I occasionally let fear get in my way. I remember this bit I did one night at The Comedy Union over on Pico. I went out onstage and asked the audience, "Y'all want to see how I would be if I was a stripper?"

People cheered and yelled back, "Hell yeah!"

I started taking my clothes off. A couple of dudes scooted forward on their chairs, adjusting their crotches, like, "I'm about to see some titties!"

But then the music kicked in. *Come and knock on our door . . .*

Dudes looked at each other like, *What the? Why is she out here looking like Run DMC dancing to* Three's Company? *Where are the titties?* One sitcom theme song after another came over the speakers while I danced. I had thought the idea of stripping to those corny songs was *hilarious* when I came up with it. But soon as I started, I could tell the audience was not on board, and that's when my fear app took over. In my head, instead of an audience having a good time, I started seeing a roomful of judges in their black robes with little hammers ready to read the verdict: This bitch is not funny. That kind of thinking will fuck you up when you are a comedian. If you start getting in your feelings about how your audience didn't laugh hard enough or how they started talking when you were onstage, you can fall into a dark hole. And your body responds. You get tentative. Timid. You lose your power.

Charles Fleischer had told me, back when I was at Comedy Camp, your body language onstage determines whether a crowd is going to listen to you or not. Whatever position you choose to put your body in, you have to commit to it 110 percent.

I was too afraid to commit once I'd seen the audience wasn't immediately with it, so I started half-assing. But for that bit to be great, I should have put my whole ass out there. *Look at what I'm working with, y'all. Watch me bounce.*

It was so awkward. No one in the audience would make eye contact with me.

And nobody laughed.

Not one person found that bit funny because I had let them get in my head. They made me doubt myself and, as a result, I hadn't committed enough to dance like I believed these were the dopest songs to dance to. If I'd had the confidence to really embody that character, it would have been fucking stellar.

But what the fuck was I so afraid of? No one there had a blowtorch. No one was pushing thumbtacks into my ass. No one was even asking for their money back. My insecurity was just my brain telling me something that was not true: that I wasn't funny and I had no right to be up on that stage. If I had let fear keep me from getting back up onstage again, that would have been the end of my career right there.

Standing on the edge of that boat, I took a look at those sharks and decided I wasn't about to let how scary they looked keep me from living my dream of diving off a boat into the clear blue water—even if it was a science boat.

The other divers were already in the water, waiting for me to join them. Adrenaline was definitely running through my system. I could hear blood whooshing in my eardrums, going, "Don't get eaten, don't get eaten," but I told myself, "Time to suit up, girl." I took off my wig and wiggled my wet suit up over my ass. I fit the snorkel on my face and told the cameras, "We about to get wet!"

I waddled over to the end of the boat in my flippers. *Flop flop flop.* And took another peek at the fins slicing up through the top of the water. I was actually here. This was really happening. The crew basically threw me off the boat. *Kaplunk.*

A billion little bubbles whited-out my mask as I adjusted to the pressure of being below the surface. When they cleared, light filtered down through the waves and lit up the water around me all sparkly. I finished equalizing and then we sank down nearly to the bottom of the ocean where the littler fish played hide-and-seek in the seaweed. The sun bounced off their scales, which was very pretty, but man, that was nothing compared to the sharks. Up close, the sharks didn't seem scary—just very, very impressive. Those were some majestic creatures, and so graceful. They didn't make any sound, just a flick of a tail and they'd glide off like an ice skater. This was their world, and I was lucky to be in it. It was so peaceful I decided to lie down on the soft sand on the ocean floor. I imagined some spa music with some chimes as a soundtrack. I got up close and personal with a few sharks, nice and friendly. The way their mouths cut across their faces made it look like they were smiling at me.

Every time my heart started to slow down, though, someone on the Shark Week team would shout through the comms, "On your left!" "Coming at you!" "Watch your back!" I'd turn around and there'd be a shark the size of an elephant coming at me. I will admit that even though I was digging these sharks, when they opened those smiles and showed me those sharp-ass teeth, there were a few times where my wet suit almost got wetter.

That night back in the hotel as the sky turned neon colors outside my window, I got in my white sheets in my white bed and fell asleep wondering how something so dangerous could be so beautiful.

A couple days later, it was time for me to cage dive. It should have been a relief knowing there would be steel bars keeping the sharks from mangling my legs, but the reason for the cage was that they were going to dangle some chopped-up fish near us so we could see a whole lot of sharks up close all at once. I know how sharks get when they eat (I had googled "feeding frenzy" before and I wasn't sure when those jaws started snapping that I wanted to be in the mix), but I was not going to let that fear stop me.

There have been times in my life where I have been in scary situations—where I have been alone asleep in my car at night, or my mom was coming after me trying to hurt me, or I was in a bad situation with a man—and I would never choose to relive those moments or wish them on anyone else. But going through all that taught me you get to choose your response when you are afraid. You might not be able to control everything that happens to you, but you do get to control how you respond to it. Are you going to let fear rule you or are you going to rule your fears?

That is what I admire about some of my favorite comedians. They refuse to let fear rule them. All the great comedians take a loss now and then. Richard Pryor bombed, Chris Rock, Wanda Sykes—everybody who is anybody has had bad sets. When you flop, you have to push through the fear that might be the last time you'll ever be on a stage, pick yourself up, dust yourself off, and try again. When the people don't laugh, that's when you grow as a comedian. You go, "Okay, this isn't right. I got to step outside my comfort zone, make adjustments. What's wrong here? Why are they not laughing? Is it my energy? My pacing? They didn't laugh when I said, 'I hope he gets hit by a taco truck.' Maybe I should say, 'I hope he gets hit by an ice cream truck' and see how that goes." You can't let fear of failure make you freeze up. It might be running in the background like that app, but instead of clicking on it, you have to swipe over to something new and go about your business.

Once I was in the water, I swam over to get inside the metal cage with a couple of the shark wranglers and the camera guys. The crew lowered the cage below the surface, and we sank from the lightest blue water down to about twenty feet, where it darkened to a deep blue. The assistants dropped chum right on top of us and sharks started showing up. At first, there were just one or two, but then one of those bad boys must have put it on blast on Shark Twitter because, all of a sudden, there were like a dozen gray bodies bumping into the metal bars, biting at them. Sharks circled all around us, trying to snap up the fish parts raining down, getting these bonito fish. There was a sign in the cage about how you should not put your body outside; I did not need a sign to tell me that. I kept my arms and legs inside the ride for sure. I swear I saw a snorkel in one of those sharks' mouths when it went in for a bite.

Our job was to count how many females and how many males we could see. There were a lot of female sharks, but there was only one small male shark. Those female sharks were boxing him out, not letting him get anything to eat, so that motha was hungry. He needed a big meal bad. Chompie made a couple of aggressive passes, whipping his tail so close that a whoosh of water rippled over my mask. Dude was sizing me up, Joker grin on his face, trying to decide if I was going to be his lunch. I did look banging in my hot pink wet suit, so I couldn't blame him for staring. But I would not let myself show any fear.

The producers at Shark Week kept coming over my earpiece, saying, "Can you pretend like you're scared?" I played along, looking over my shoulders and making the big eyes—like *Ohmigod, I'm about to get gobbled up by this bull shark! Somebody help!*—because I am an actor and that's my job. But I was not scared.

At some level, I knew there was an element of danger while I was in that cage because the type of sharks we were with, they could get up to five hundred pounds, and sometimes they do eat people. Sharks have these sensors in their snouts. I forget the name of them. It sounds like an Italian dish, like "Ana Linguini" or something. (I just googled it. It's called "ampullae of Lorenzini.") That sensor tells them how fast your heart is beating, which lets them know if you're scared. If you're scrambling, trying to get out of the cage, freaking out, hiding, they can smell that fear, and they will come for you. They are looking for the weak, someone who lets fear take over.

And that was not me. Like I told the producers, swimming with sharks wasn't any different from walking around my hood at night. You just had to look those sharks in their beady little eyes and tell them who's boss.

I was in control of my response. I chose to set fear aside and be able to experience something amazing.

That's what happens when you set yourself free from fear—you live your life better. You can actually participate in life—do what you were put on this earth to do.

Once I learned to stop giving so big a fuck about whether I was going to bomb or if the audience was going to like me and started just going for it onstage, my comedy got stronger. (I'll tell you how I managed to find my swagger in the next chapter.) It was like a self-fulfilling prophecy. I got to a certain level of confidence in myself, and the audience could feel it. It's like they believed I could do no wrong. When I am feeling no fear, I could cut my toenails during a set, and the audience will be like, "Yo, yo, you cutting your nails! That's *hilarious*." You just have to own it, and not worry so much about what the audience is going to think about your set.

When my dog Dreamer died on the first day of 2022, I was crushed. I'd had that dog for thirteen years. That was my bitch, my protector. She let me know who I could trust and who was hustling me. The week after she died, I got onstage. I was so upset that I put any fear that the audience wouldn't like it if I talked about my dog out of my head.

I went, *I don't care what y'all think. Y'all can all get up and walk out right now. I'm going to talk about what I want to talk about.* So, I talked about my dog for twenty-five minutes straight. I told the audience how my Black friends were like, "Sorry your dog died. When you going to get another one?" while my white friends were like, "Oh my god, Tiffany. How are you holding up? I'm *so* upset. Do you need anything? Can I bring you a casserole? What are you going to do with the dog food? Can I have it?"

I was trying not to cry in front of these people while I told them about how Dreamer used to watch me have sex, how she used to vet guys for me, sleep in the bed with me when there was no man there— all our journeys together. I spoke straight from the heart. I didn't let fear stop me from being open and vulnerable. I just let it all hang out.

I fucking demolished. I ripped it. It was an amazing set. I was so in it, I didn't even see any faces. I knew they were laughing. I could hear them. But I was not performing for them; I was performing for me.

That's the ticket: When you're not scared, you're not thinking about what other people think of you. You're just presenting your full self. That's when the jokes are flying. The only thing I'ma worry about is my high heels breaking onstage.

Next time he swam by me in my cage, I looked that male shark in the eye, like, *All right, Chompie, come at me. See what happens.*

He looked at me and went, "Oh no. I'm not about to eat this cocky-looking sea turtle. She's too tough. Probably gonna taste like metal anyway." Then off he swam to find him a mermaid.

Listen, the world can be fucking scary. Watching the news on the wrong day, I'm sucking my thumb again. But I cannot let fear hold me back. I know if I do that, I am going to end up being one of those mole people who only leave the house to take out the trash. If I had let my fear of getting eaten alive take over, I never would have experienced those amazing moments of peace and beauty at the bottom of the sea. Whenever fear sneaks in, I allow myself to feel fifteen minutes of anxiety. I set a timer and when it goes off—*boop boop boop boop*—it's time to shut down the app. I've got things to do. Life to live. I'm gonna call a man about a yacht.

BIG TIFF ENERGY

I HAD A DICK for a week, and it changed my life.

Let me explain.

The first part of my twenties, I was trying to figure out how to carry myself and how to be in the world, including how I looked. Like you do in your twenties. I went around in super-tight clothes that looked like they were painted on. I always had my belly out like I was in an Xzibit video to show where I got my belly button pierced. This was back in the early 2000s and I was working at the ticket counter at an airline with a mess of white women and a few Hispanic and Black women. I'd drive from South Central to LAX and roll in there looking flossy, repping Floss Angeles.

Whenever we had a break between flights, these ladies liked to give me advice. They told my hood ass, "You should try to be more sophisticated, Tiffany. You have to do this. You have to do that." Seemed to me like some of them had their lives together—with husbands and homes and shit—so I listened to what they were saying. I tried a bunch of different things they'd suggested so I could appear to be more of an adult and be taken more seriously. I wore contacts—green contacts, blue contacts—and put on this blue eye shadow all over my eyelids. I changed my hair. I wore Afros for a little while, then later, I got my first weave. It was not a great weave. When I went to the salon, bitch pulled my hair so tight, the weave came with a free facelift.

After work, I'd go out dancing with my friends, and damn, did I get a lot of attention in the clubs. Dudes pushed up on me while I danced, trying to talk to me.

"Oh, you cute. What you doing later, girl?"

But you know what? It felt like shit because that look I'd put together based on other people's advice, it wasn't me. Even though I was getting noticed, I always felt like I was in a costume.

Right around the time I started sporting that "sophisticated" look, my comedy career was stalling out. The feedback I was getting was confusing as hell. I'd walk offstage in my getup, and male comics would come up to me and say, "You're a pretty girl, but you so ghetto. Why don't you try to be a little more sophisticated in what you say onstage? All you got is dick jokes." I wanted to say, "Have you seen a dick? And you don't want to make a joke about it? You are stronger than I am."

It was like they couldn't get their heads around the existence of a woman who wasn't super polite and polished. I have noticed that Black women get pressured to try to fit into a mold, do the Clair Huxtable, be the epitome of Black excellence. But I am not Clair Huxtable. Where I come from, we're loud, we clap, we point fingers, we reach out and snatch your soul. When we're happy, we're happy; when we're mad, we're mad; when we're sad, we're sad. And we are going to let you know it. A lot of us are not shy about talking about sex, but a lot of times, that makes other people uncomfortable. Fact was, I did talk about sex in my act, but I wasn't *just* talking about sex. I was talking about my childhood, talking about my family, talking about working at the airlines, all of that, but the jokes weren't landing.

I wasn't getting gigs. I constantly got bumped off lineups. Bookers would say, "Oh, yeah. Come do this show. You can go on at eleven thirty." I'd drive all the way across town to some poorly lit establishment in the middle of nowhere—barely had any gas in my car 'cause I was broke—and when I arrived, they'd say, "Ah, on second thought, we ain't going to pay you." Or, "Nah, we ain't got no spot for you after all. There's two other females here, so you're not going to be on."

What the hell?

What I didn't realize is that they were responding to the fact that I wasn't one thing or the other. I wasn't the proper lady from the airlines, and I wasn't relaxed into my true self. I was presenting this sophisticated look, but then I was telling jokes as dirty as I liked but without an authentic, fully-me delivery. It was fake as fuck, secondhand news.

Being fake is very, very destructive. It sucks your soul, sets you back, steals your joy. People were not seeing the real me because I was hiding behind those clothes. I was also hiding myself onstage. I mean that literally *and* figuratively. I would try to make myself as small as possible behind the mic stand, like in cartoons where Bugs Bunny would suck in his gut to hide behind a telephone pole.

Now I know that if you want people to laugh at you up on that stage, you can't hide. You have to be your full self, your real self. Took me a while to learn that, which is why I did what I did next.

I couldn't help but notice other comics weren't getting turned away when they showed up at gigs—not even comics with the same amount of experience as me. I looked around and saw who was getting most of the gigs and who was not being disrespected: It was the men. They were booking shows. They weren't hiding behind the mic. They were letting it all hang out, talking about whatever the fuck they wanted to talk about onstage. Wasn't that something?

I thought, *That is fucked up. I know I am as funny as these dudes. I could get as many laughs as they do if I could just get the stage time. Here's what I'm going to do. I'll wear these knockoff Kangol hats that everybody's fronting. Some jeans, tank tops. I'm going to look like a man and then maybe I'll get respected like one.*

And that's what I did. I took off my airline lady look and put on this zip-up red sweater with a hood as my go-to item of clothing. I'd wear that Little Red Riding Hood sweater with a leather jacket on top. I'd get my combat boots on, my black Doc Martens, and you could not tell me I was not funny.

I was hanging out with Marlo Williams a lot back then, and she gave me hella shit for my man look.

"What are you doing? If you not gay, why are you dressing like this?"

"Because I want bookers to get me up onstage so people can hear my jokes."

"Bitch, they're too confused about what you got on to listen to your jokes. Are you a comic or do you play basketball? Are you telling jokes or are you working at a construction site?"

I'd just tell her, "Shut up, Marlo. Give me the weed."

She wasn't wrong. I didn't just dress like a man, I tried to talk like them, to get in their heads, to act like them. I'd watch them at different comedy spots, how they carried themselves, taking note of their every move, how they held themselves, how they smoked, how they laughed, their big dick energy. I was like an anthropologist studying the species *manus bigdickus.*

For three or four years, I tried to keep it boyish so people would actually listen to me and not sexualize me. Look at me for what I had to say, not necessarily pay attention to my body. But it wasn't working. I might have been wearing the clothes, but I didn't have that energy that said, "Yo, listen up. Pay attention." Because I was still faking it.

People think it's easy to be fake 'cause it takes less work to follow what someone else is doing instead of being yourself, but no. It's *uncomfortable* not being you. It's like you're dragging your ass around in a meat suit that fits bad. This is why actors get paid what they get paid. It is taxing to keep up a façade.

One night, I was doing The Hop in Lakewood. It was late, and I felt like crap. This lady came up to me while I was with Marlo. She was an older Black woman with auburn hair and Lee press-on French nails. I guess she had worked with some entertainers back in the seventies and eighties, and she still stayed part of the scene. She put her hand on her hip, looked me in the face, and said, "You got a lot of talent, but the way you dress, you ain't never going to get nowhere."

"What?" I looked down at my baggy-ass jeans. Looked okay to me.

"Let me tell you something. You cute. You got a nice little shape, but you trying to hide it. Stop hiding it. You a woman. That's your advantage over these men. Wear some cute jeans. Let your arms be out. Do you got flabby arms? Let me see your arms." I took my jacket off, so she could see my arms.

"You got nice arms. I bet you got pretty legs, too. Wear some shorts. Wear a dress. Put on some damn makeup—some real makeup. Get some mascara, some blush, some lips, lashes. And comb your hair. Don't come out the house with your hair not combed."

"I *did* comb my hair."

"Well, why you got that ugly-ass hat on your head if you combed your hair?"

When we got in the car, Marlo said, "That bitch didn't tell not one goddamn lie. I've been trying to tell your ass to put on some motherfucking heels."

So I was like, *These hos might be right. I need to start being more feminine again. But not like those airline bitches told me. Like what makes me feel sexy and powerful.*

Angelina Jolie's *Tomb Raider* had just come out, so I decided to try out that *Tomb Raider* look because it felt like I could fight if I needed to fight when I was rocking that look, but it was still sexy. I took off my Little Red Riding hoodie, put away my off-brand hats and baggy jeans, and put together a look that was feminine and powerful—some heels, a shirt that let my belly button ring show again, green army fatigues, little side satchel. I had my hair braided up in a ponytail, earrings, a little star necklace on my neck. It felt natural. It felt like *me*.

Onstage, I started loosening up, roaming around more, doing the jokes I wanted to do without caring if they were the right jokes for a lady. Don't you know, I started booking more gigs. When I showed up looking like Lara Croft, instead of turning me away at the door, bookers would put me on. I even made it into the *Los Angeles Times* when I did a show for the veterans.

There was power in that look, like I was on some hero crusade, setting off booby traps before they could catch me. I could break any curse, conquer any obstacle, solve any puzzle—including the Rubik's Cube of how to make it as a Black woman in the comedy business. I was feeling myself. Things were actually starting to go pretty good.

But then my life took a turn for the worse.

This is a whole dark, depressing-as-fuck story that I don't want to get into right now. All you need to know is I tried to turn my energy down, be something for someone else I was not, and it fucking sucked. In that period of my life, it wasn't just that I wasn't dressing like my real self; I wasn't *being* my real self.

That was the most depressed time I have ever had. I've never cried so much, never hated myself so much. I was working so hard on being something I wasn't just to please another person, and it was exhausting. My energy, my life force, was drained to nothing. I was living completely without joy. And I became so angry.

I'd been acting like this other version of myself for so long, I didn't know who the fuck I was anymore. I had a million questions. Could I go back to where I was five years ago? What was I? I knew I was a comedian, but what kind of comedian? Was I a dirty comic? Is that what I wanted to be—the dick joke–telling comic? Or did I want to be the clean comic who's respected? I'd record these questions for myself into my cell phone and then try to answer them the next day. It was a real soul-searching time.

Which brings me to my dick.

What happened was I did this podcast, and they gave me a gift bag after the show. It was full of sexy stuff—vibrators, tubes of lube, and this fleshy limp dick, like an old pink cucumber. I was like, *What the fuck I'm going to do with this?*

On the podcast, we'd been talking about women who strap on and walk around with a fake penis between their legs. Obviously, people do that for all sorts of reasons, but as a straight chick, that had never been my bag . . . yet. That night, I looked down at the limp fake penis I had in my hand and went, *Hmm.*

The next day when I got dressed for the set I was going to do at the Laugh Factory, I found a pair of bigger pants in my closet and I slid that flaccid penis right into my panties. It felt weird to have something stuck in the front of my coochie hairs. There was a little bulge, but the pants were roomy, so from the outside, you couldn't really *tell* tell. But with that dick in there, I walked different. To accommodate it, I had to add a swagger when I rolled up to the front of the room to get onstage for my set. I spread my legs a little wider when I stood up onstage, took up more space. My body felt good. *Hell, yeah. I should take up more space.* Something about wearing that dick pushed a button inside, opened up a cage door, and Tiffany came bounding out. I felt like I could be as big and loud and too much as I wanted, which felt amazing after years of trying to make myself smaller. Confidence rolled through me and came out in my delivery.

Wearing that dick onstage, I felt like I was doing the Care Bear stare at the audience, chest out like, *Yeah! Jokes jokes jokes.*

The audience was laughing so hard you could see their teeth. I love to hear those big *Ha ha ha*s because when you laugh, it lights you up. I finally had that big dick energy. No. Fuck that, I had that *Big Tiff Energy.*

I kept that penis in my panties for a whole week. When I wore dresses, I put some shorts on because I didn't want it to fall out onstage like I was shitting dildos. Everywhere I went, people couldn't wait to talk to me. People were respecting me. They weren't trying to talk to me or calling me, "Hey, little sis." They were saying *Tiffany.* After my sets, dudes would come up. "Yo, I got this club. You want to come do this spot?" Or, "Tiff. I'm writing on this show. I would love for you to audition for it." What the hell? Could they tell I got a dick?

In that one week, I booked fifteen gigs.

After those seven days, I got rid of my fake dick. But I decided *I'm going to keep this walk. That energy.*

I remembered what the late great Bob Saget said to me one night at the Laugh Factory. The owner of the club, Jamie Masada, had come over to chew me out after a set I'd done that had a lot of dick jokes in it, saying, "You can't be cussing onstage like that. You should be a clean comedian."

Bob overheard what Jamie had said. After Jamie left, he gave me a kiss on the forehead and said, "Fuck that. Do not let them change who you are. If you feel good doing it, that's what you need to be doing." He wanted me to know I should just be me.

Once I loosened up, I *felt* more like me. It was like my soul was being seen under my clothes. No one was repressing my spirit, telling me how to be. I was moving through the world more like men—entitled to be themselves, no one judging them, no matter how loud or assertive they are or how much space they take up.

I decided I'd rather people go, "She so loud. I don't want to be around her," or "She too hyper . . . too much energy for me," than turn myself off to accommodate others or make them feel more comfortable in my presence.

So many people in the Black community have said I'm destroying the community by being myself. They say I'm cooning, setting our people back a hundred years. Are you kidding me? A hundred years ago, I would have gotten killed for speaking my mind. I hear, "You're perpetuating stereotypes, Tiffany." Well, it's not like I was raised in the suburbs and my mom and dad were doctors and lawyers. Bitch, I come from the goddamn streets. I am a stereotype. I put the "type" in the motherfucking stereo. Somebody typed on that shit, and it spit my ass out.

I started telling as many dick jokes as I felt like, cussing when it was called for—or even just because I fucking felt like it. I became a very physical comedian, using the whole stage when I performed. I mugged, I strutted around, I shook my booty, I got down on the ground and popped back up again—all in thirty seconds. It was like I'd been blocking joy with all that fakeness I'd put out there. Now I know when I line up the me I let people see with the real me, the chute is clear and the joy flows freely out of me.

The more I allowed myself to be Tiffany Haddish, the more people liked me, the more they wanted to help me, and the more opportunities presented themselves. They saw the joy flowing when I was being real and they wanted some for themselves. I was more than happy to share.

The key to life is: Be yourself. That's how you win. Everybody ain't gonna like you. You're not gonna please everybody. Everybody ain't gonna respect you. But it's a waste of energy to constantly ask yourself, "Should I be like this? Should I act like that?" when you should just be you. Don't try to be the girl you see on IG. Don't try to be me. Just be you. Being you saves you from a whole lotta stress.

When people are like, "I can't stand Tiffany Haddish. I don't like how she out here living her life," I want to tell them, "You mad because you fake. You mad because you're not being yourself. You mad because you're really a piece of shit and you're trying to act like you're not a piece of shit. Maybe if you just be the piece of shit that you are, you might be fun, and people would want to be around you."

I'm not gonna lie, when you go full you and you don't apologize for it, there are going to be haters who get fired up about it. That's part of being cursed with joy. Some jealous mofos might try to bring you down. But you don't ever, ever, ever turn your light off or turn your spirit down. If you're loud, be loud. If you're quiet, be quiet. What is comfortable and real for you is where you should be.

I talk how I talk. I dress how I dress. I am who I am. I honor that. You try to make me something I'm not, and I walk away. Big Tiff Energy in every step.

LIVE FROM NEW YORK

I HAVE ACCOMPLISHED A lot in my life so far—I can cook a good brisket, I am an excellent gardener, and I will whup your ass in a footrace—but I have a mess of goals I'd still like to meet. For one thing, I'm starting a grocery store in my neighborhood where we can sell food and other products that come exclusively from Black vendors. I'm going to call it Diaspora Groceries. I also want to start a youth center where young people can learn financial literacy and life skills, like how to cook delicious meals that are good for them. And . . . I am in the process of learning to do the splits. I can reliably get to where I am about five inches off the ground, but certain days I can get my coochie to kiss the floor. I need that to happen every day. I've been working on it. I do fifteen minutes of stretching each morning, pulling at my groin, straining 'til it screams at me. Sometimes you need to go through a little pain to get to where you want to be. Once I can do a full split on demand, when I get with a man, I'ma hit him with the Haddish. *BAM!* All the way down. He's going to have to be strong in the back to support me.

But my biggest goal, my purpose here on earth, has always been to spend as much time as I can making jokes in front of a live audience. Being onstage feels like being home. When I'm up there doing my set, that's my calling. The way priests feel called to preach and serve the Lord? I feel called to make people laugh. That audience is my congregation, and I am there to lift their spirits. I never needed to be famous. I don't do what I do for trophies or money. Well, okay, no, that's not true. I do like the money. I got to get that generational wealth. But when it comes down to it, I just want to be successful at doing stand-up comedy. That's it.

Being an entertainer is in my blood. A bunch of my family are artists and entertainers. My grandmother was hella cool. She was one of the first Black women to be on TV modeling clothes, and she also acted in plays. My grandfather was in a doo-wop group called the Titans. You can find a video on YouTube of him and his band singing. He's there in his bow tie, snapping his fingers and singing, "It's so hard to laugh, so easy to cry, now that we've said goodbye." They were going to be a big deal, but the leader of the group got caught sleeping with the chief of police's daughter, and LAPD don't play, so dude disappeared right before their big gig in Vegas that was going to launch them. The band ended up breaking up, but my grandfather stayed in entertainment anyway. He opened a theatre in New York City. My grandfather's sister has a dance school in Nevada. One auntie is a singer. My other auntie was a dancer. My mom wanted to be a fashion designer. My daddy, he was a disappearing artist. Pretty much my whole family is in arts and entertainment, so it's like I was destined to be, too.

As I was coming up in comedy, I figured out that if you want to make more money as a comic, then you got to get on TV to get more asses in seats when you do shows. I got it in my head that the best way to do that was to be on *Saturday Night Live*. *SNL* is an institution, and I liked the idea of being on a show where talented people could go to grow, to work out their material and become great. Being on a sketch comedy show seemed better than doing a sitcom because on a sketch show you get to be different characters each week. You don't get stuck doing the same role over and over. I remember Jaleel White talking about how, after *Family Matters,* he got stuck in a Steve Urkel box. Urkel is funny as hell, but that sucked for Jaleel 'cause he wanted to do more than just put on some glasses, hitch up his pants, and go, "Did I do that?" At *SNL,* you mix it up. One week, you're in a shark suit; next week, you're doing Black Jeopardy.

In the early 2000s, I got an opportunity to try to get on *Saturday Night Live.* The Laugh Factory over on Sunset hosted a showcase where we had to do a few characters in front of somebody who went around the US scouting for the show.

I was prepared. I'd been watching the show ever since I heard about it as a nine-year-old kid. I used to bring home VHS tapes from the library. My grandma had a bunch of videos at home of Red Skelton, some Carol Burnett, some Dean Martin. I liked watching the singing and dancing, but what I loved most was when the actors would break character for a second—they'd either make a mistake, flub a line or miss a cue, or find the other actors' performance so funny they'd be cracking up. Couldn't keep a straight face. You could see they were having fun. I loved to watch those shows with my grandma, but she didn't have any old *SNL.* So, I went to the library over to where they had videotapes and found the *Saturday Night Live* section. I started at the beginning of the shelf. Season one, episode one.

I put the cassette in the VCR and sat down in front of the TV, sucking on my thumb as I watched season after season. I saw John Belushi, Dan Aykroyd, and, of course, Garrett Morris—the only Black actor on the damn show in the early years.

Now, a lot of comedians will tell you that watching *SNL* was like going to church for them growing up. They never missed a single week because they just found it so damn funny. I wouldn't say that was the case for me. I wasn't watching it going, "Ha, ha, ha, ha." It was more like *Hmmmmmm*. I knew the show was supposed to be *hilarious*, but I wasn't really laughing out loud when I watched it. I was *interested* in the sketches like the way I am interested in looking at slides under my microscope. I treated each joke like a specimen, dissecting what made it work. This chubby man waving around a samurai sword or this tall skinny dude singing about King Tut—people thought that was funny? Okay. Good to know.

Personally, I would rather watch Fire Marshall Bill or Wanda on *In Living Color* or pretty much any episode of *Arsenio* than those sketches, but it was good information for me to have.

I started to find *Saturday Night Live* funny sometime in the nineties. That was when it seemed like everyone around me was talking about it, quoting it, impersonating it when we played improv games during Comedy Sports at school. We would be doing a scene, and someone would bust out with Dana Carvey's *Turtle, turrr-tle*. Fucking copycats.

That was the era of bits like Night at Roxbury and Superstar, when legends like Will Ferrell, Adam Sandler, David Spade, and Molly Shannon were on the cast. Oh, and Chris Farley. You have to remember this was when I was at the white high school, where every dude in a baseball hat thought Chris Farley was the most hilarious thing they'd ever seen. And I actually agreed. That man could stir soup and I would have laughed my ass off. Of course, I kept a close eye on the few Black actors on the show, like Tim Meadows—and Chris Rock, though I blinked and he was gone. Black women were nowhere to be seen.

Those were the years I was working as a hype man at bar mitzvahs. When I entered the system, I'd come back after a night firing up the bubbies and I'd roll into the group home in time for the show's cold open. I'd change the channel to NBC and the room would explode in protest. You have no idea how hard it is to get a bunch of Black and Hispanic kids to watch *SNL*. Trying to convince them that Garth was as funny as Homie the Clown? That was a problem. I almost got stabbed twice, y'all.

I had all the sketches I'd watched over the years—the Spartan Cheerleaders, Eddie Murphy's Gumby, the Church Lady—in my head when I got up onstage at the Laugh Factory to try to join the cast. I gave it my all, like I always do, because entertaining is what I do best.

I did a set with some new characters. In retrospect, some of them might have been kinda inappropriate, but at least I had committed.

After that showcase, nothing happened. No call offering me the job. No contract. I couldn't see it then, but that was the universe telling me, *This isn't for you, girl.*

A lot of times when we are headed toward our destiny, we take a wrong turn. When that happens, the universe will find a way to tell us, *Turn around, dummy. Do not enter. You go this way, you're gonna get run over by an eighteen-wheeler.* That rejection is a message, a gift, but we can be real pigheaded sometimes.

My career was actually going pretty good, at least in terms of getting stage time, even if I didn't get paid a lot. I was booking gigs in some of the bigger clubs even without being a cast member on *SNL*, but I couldn't shake the idea that that show was my path. Granted, they had made it very clear they didn't want me, but I said to myself, "Oh, you a quitter? I don't think so. You got to get some name recognition or you're going to be nobody for the rest of your life. Get back out there."

So, a few years later in 2010 when my agent told me *SNL* was looking for new cast members, I made an audition tape. They asked me to prepare five characters—three original characters and two celebrities. And you'd best make it funny. I remember I did Vivica Fox and my version of Suze Orman. I played her like a ghetto financial adviser. "You have to pay yourself first. Those first ten food stamps are for you!"

Word came back that the producers had liked what they'd seen. They were going to fly me out to New York to audition for Lorne Michaels and the rest of the producers and executives. Well, hot diggity damn! No one had ever flown me anywhere to try out for a job before.

Now, I love auditions. That's an opportunity for me to play, to be super creative, to shake a little Haddish at 'em. I give every audition my all—even if it's to be a model at a swap meet—because that might be my last chance to ever perform. As far as I'm concerned, every opportunity is the best opportunity.

I have certainly had some bad auditions. In fact, I've had auditions where I thought I might get arrested 'cause I did not like how things went down. One time, this casting director was going in on me about not looking like my headshot. She told me it was horrible because I didn't send a full body shot, just a bust. She was upset that I didn't look like my photo 'cause I came in jeans and not what I was wearing in my picture. She expected me to be just a head in a dress? No legs, just walking in on my titties? I did not get that part, but I also did not slap the dogshit out of that casting director, so I count it as a win.

Other auditions have not gone well because I went for the wrong parts. One studio had me in for a role that called for a girl with blue eyes and blond hair who was very voluptuous. I put on a blond wig, blue contacts, and I stuffed my bra full of tissues 'til I was like a lumpy Black Pamela Anderson. They ended up going in a different direction.

On the day of my New York audition for *SNL*, I was ready. I walked in there telling myself, like I do, "Tiffany Haddish, they love and approve of you," 'cause however you feel when you walk into that door, that's how they'll feel about you. You've got to remind yourself they need *you*; they called *you* in. You're just there to be of service. You're doing them a favor by even showing up.

I walked into the studio and took pictures of everything and everybody with my little disposable camera, all like, "I'm about to be on *Saturday Night Live!*" It's hard to say why I cared so much about getting on the show. I guess it's just that *SNL* was like the litmus test of whether you were considered funny or not by the comedy establishment. I wonder if even the best jazz musicians are secretly side-eyeing classical musicians and wondering if people would see them as more legit if they would just fucking play a little Mozart now and again. Whether or not the show was actually funny didn't factor in. It was that it was seen as the big leagues, an official "certified funny" on the back of your headshot for life.

I took pictures of the set, the crew, the craft services table. I even took a picture with the janitor because he was the only Black person I saw there besides Kenan. After makeup and wardrobe check, they sent me into the dressing rooms in the back to wait to be called.

I warmed up, stretched out my tongue, shook out my shoulders. Then I sat in my chair, getting my face moving, going "Baby daddy, baby daddy, baby daddy, baby daddy, child support, child support, child support." Because I like to say what I don't want really fast, so I can get what I do want when I audition.

There were about twenty of us there, and I was the only Black woman. That waiting room was like something out of *Cinderella*, everybody crossing their fingers that they were going to be the right fit. When it was my turn, I kicked things off with an original character, Gladys, a phone sex operator with a hole in her throat from where she had smoked too much. I stood in front of those old white dudes and made like I was using one of those voice boxes: "Hey, big boy, you want to play?" They loved it.

The laughs only got bigger after that. Every bit I did set them off. I knocked it out of the damn park.

As I was leaving, I was in the elevator with a couple of the guys that handle the set design. One guy in a jangly old tool belt said, "You're very funny, but they're not going to have you on the show."

What? I had *killed it* back there. He was just hating. I tucked my camera back in my bag and said, "Yeah, whatever. I'll see you next season."

What I hadn't put together until my agent called me was this old guy was one of the dudes who was controlling the lights up in the rafters. He knew the ins and outs of the show and what they were looking for. I didn't get the job. Again. The universe was like, "How many times do I have to tell you? This isn't for you. Now get your ass back onstage and tell some damn jokes."

Because I'm a good listener, I went back to LA and got onstage every chance I got. Five, six, seven nights a week. I was up there making people laugh those big belly laughs with material I'd worked on from my life. I loved it. Every time I performed, I felt that rush, that immediate gratification, and there's nothing like it. But in the back of my mind, a little voice was still buzzing around like, "Damn, you're funny. You know, you sure would be good on *Saturday Night Live*."

In 2014, my homeboy Finesse, who used to work on *SNL*, told me they were going to host auditions for a Black female cast member. They might as well have sent a written invitation: "Tiffany Haddish, here's your chance, girl. Come on out." He said it was going to be like ten girls trying out at the Groundlings Theatre in LA, and I should give it a shot. I decided to give it one last try.

I showed up expecting an intimate audition in front of a few people, but it turned out it was a full comedy show with an audience. All the other women had brought their crews to support them while I was rolling solo. I had just flown back into town after doing the *Dirty Sexy Funny* show with Jenny McCarthy, so I was already kind of exhausted. Then I got a flat tire, and now I was finding out that I could have had fans there to support me? Not great. Might not have been my best audition, but I did the best I could considering the circumstances. Turns out, it didn't matter. None of those other actresses got cast either, friends in the audience or not. The producers already knew who they wanted to cast.

I got some heat for talking about this with *TMZ*. They called me while I was trying to get my tire fixed, and I told them this audition was a waste of Black women's time and gas money. They translated that into me calling the whole deal a "publicity stunt." I probably should not have picked up that call. Noted, universe.

You might already know I finally got my chance to be on the show after *Girls Trip* came out. In 2017, I got a call from my manager asking me if I wanted to host. Did I want to host the show I'd been trying to get on for more than ten years? Hell yeah, I wanted to do it. Abso-fucking-lutely. Sign me up.

You might be thinking, *So the universe was wrong. You were meant to be on that show after all.* Well, kind of.

When the time came, I was not nervous. I was excited. I wanted to do it right, so I did what I always do to get ready: research. I called all the legends, the best of the best, to get advice. I called Whoopi Goldberg to ask her for some wisdom about how to host. She said, "Oh, girl, I never hosted."

"What do you mean? Yes, you did. I saw you on there."

"No, I did one sketch with Billy Crystal. I wasn't the host. You the first. Don't fuck it up."

I love Whoopi, but I thought maybe she didn't have her facts right. Wanda Sykes had to have done it. I called Wanda, but she said, "Nope, haven't done it."

I googled it. I went through all the archives, all the episodes, but Whoopi was right. I was going to be the first Black female comic to host the show. I'd always wanted to be the first person to do something. I'd thought maybe I was going to be the first Black woman to get to ride a unicorn in a movie instead of those pasty wood nymphs they usually show, not hosting *SNL*, but I'd take it. *Booyah!*

I knew being the first meant I had to bring it. On Monday, when it was time to get started, I came into the studio with my energy out of the roof and a notebook full of ideas. I had four or five sketches outlined and ready to go. I went into the writers' room and handed them my notebook. "*Ta-dow!* These are the jokes, guys. This is what I want to do. When do we start?"

They were all quiet for a second. They were very polite when they slid my notebook back to me across the table like, *Thank you for being prepared, but it don't work like that, baby girl. We got this.*

Hold up, hold up. I had finally made it to the show, and my ideas were getting shot down right out the gate? Why are you blocking me, God?

I probably should've just sat my ass down, but instead I said to myself, "Let me try one more time." I picked up my notebook and told them, "Let me show you this one thing . . ."

I left the writers' room and got back to rehearsing, but having my shit turned down flat-out didn't sit right with me. We worked on the writers' sketches until three o'clock in the morning. I was cooperating, reading the Boo Boo Jeffries character, going "Ree-ah-nah, Ree-ah-nah. Beyoncé, Beyoncé." But in my mind, I was still thinking about how good *my* sketches were.

I enjoy working with others. I love working with creative people to make something fun and funny or dramatic and heart-wrenching by collaborating. But deep down, I like my ideas best. Maybe I'm narcissistic that way, but it's part of what I love about doing stand-up. It's what *I* wrote, what *I* want to do, who *I* am. I am called to share that with the world.

I came back at the writers on Tuesday with my notebook, asking, "What do you mean you're not going to look at these jokes? This is great stuff!"

Again, they said—a little less patiently this time—"We really don't need your sketches, Tiffany. You just focus on your monologue."

I blinked at the writers. Slowly, I started to realize it was not going to go like I thought. I thought I was destined to be part of this show, but *Saturday Night Live* was a machine that'd been running for forty-plus years. Me thinking I could roll in with what I wanted to do, I must have been out of my mind. I was nothing but a little squirt of oil to help that machine keep going.

I was pissed because I felt like I should have some say over what I was about to be a part of. Everything I do has a lot of heart in it and a whole lot of Tiffany in it, too. I didn't have to fight every fight, but I wasn't going to put my name on something that didn't have my stamp on it. Could be that I am a little bit of a control freak because I had to be in control of my own life since I was really young. Either way, I wasn't giving up. We were there until all hours of the night the whole week.

Over the course of those long-ass hours, in between rehearsing my parts and trying to memorize my lines and getting fitted for wardrobe and makeup, I talked to every single writer of every sketch until I wore them down so one or two of my jokes or ideas could get in it. Eventually, I did get tidbits into every single sketch. I got some Tiffany Haddish in there.

The last two days I was on set, I decided that tidbits were good, but I needed more. I was gonna bring the full force of Tiffany Haddish in the monologue.

That was the one part of the show that was all mine, so it needed to be fire. The producers had told me I could say or do whatever I wanted. I had watched a lot of monologues and wanted to make sure I was on point. I put blood, sweat, and tears in, trying to get it to sound like me and be funny as hell. It was a little sexy, a little vulnerable. A lot excited. I put a little Japanese in it 'cause I had just learned to speak some. I wrote the script out and handed it over. "Here you go." The producers took a look and said, "Well, let's see. You can't say this." X out. "And you definitely can't say that." Crossed that out.

"What is this? Japanese? You can't put that in here. That's just going to confuse middle America. Not going to happen."

Wait a minute. Amy Schumer was out there talking about her vagina for three minutes, and I can't say *konichiwa*? I decided I shouldn't trip. I'd be a professional. I'd take the notes. But I was still going to get my message across. I'd do my thing even if it was within certain parameters. "All right," I said, "I'll be in your little box, but I will be the brightest light you ever saw in there. I'm gonna shine all over your damn stage." For those six minutes, I was going to bring the Haddish. I was going to wear my best dress. I was going to joke about foster care. I was going to do some praise and worship dancing. Thing is, people can only box you in so much if you're doing what the Lord put you here to do, and He put me here to bring joy.

The night of the show was a dream come true—just not in the way I'd thought it would be. Once I saw what it was like to work in Studio 8H, I finally understood I was not meant to be on that show. I might not have been shoved in a box if I'd become a cast member, but I would never have gotten to be full-on Tiffany. Uncut. I am grateful that Lorne Michaels never hired me because I would not have made it in that work environment. You have to be a special type of beast to handle that. I am made to be Tiffany Haddish, stand-up comedian. One week was fine, but I lost ten pounds in those seven days. That's how stressed out I was. A couple weeks of that and I would have looked like a praying mantis.

Anytime someone tells me "no," I've got a choice. I could choose to see that "no" as a dead end, or I could choose to keep going, to trust in my destiny. If something doesn't pan out, then I know it wasn't meant to be. I wasn't meant to do those sketches from my notebook on *SNL*. Now I can use them somewhere else for myself.

Thank you, Lorne, for showing me the door. For passing on me, for telling me no freaking way was I going to be a cast member. My rejection was my protection.

Things line up in life to get you where you are. If something doesn't go your way, maybe it wasn't meant to. I've learned to listen to "no." If I missed out on it, I guess it wasn't for me. I wasn't supposed to be part of that anyway. If you say no, someone else is going to say yes and I need to be able to have space in my life for that.

Here's what's real: That night I got to host was absolutely magical. First Black female comedian—I did that. I made that history. I won a goddamn Emmy. I looked fly as hell in my Alexander McQueen dress, I hit my marks, and I nailed my lines, but I *slayed* my monologue. Because that monologue was me. I was at home up there. And there's no place like home.

ELELELE

THIS IS THE STORY of my Oscar dress—and how I almost knocked a motherfucker out over it.

Everybody knows the Oscars is like the Super Bowl for actors' fashion. You bring your A-game when you're flexin' on that red carpet. That's the moment. That's where you make your mark. For an actress, your dress is everything.

I got my invite to the ceremony in 2018, the year after *Girls Trip* came out. I had gone to awards shows before, but this was the *big* show, the flashiest fashion moment of my career. I had a stylist—let's call him Tiddlywinks—I'd worked with for a while, and it was going to be his job to get me red-carpet ready. We got along well 'cause he grew up in South Central, too, so we shared a background and a certain sensibility. Plus, Tiddlywinks was a lot of fun to be around. He's funny, goofy, and very stylish. We used to go to clubs, getting turnt and dancing late into the night. We even did a painting class together one time. I just liked spending time with him. He's about my size and has that masculine and feminine energy. In the '90s, you would have said he was a metrosexual.

Dressing someone for the Oscars is huge for a stylist, and Tiddlywinks knew he had to nail it. After weeks of phone calls and discussions, he came over to my house very excited because he had managed to arrange for Brandon Maxwell to design a dress for me. Brandon is an amazing designer who had worked with Lady Gaga, Viola Davis, and Kerry Washington. As much as I appreciated all the effort my stylist had put in getting Brandon lined up, I had a different dress in mind to wear to the event: my Eritrean princess dress.

I'd gotten it when I visited Eritrea for the first time. It was the fall of 2017, six months after my dad died. I was there to put his ashes to rest beside his mother's. Losing my dad was insanely painful for me. He left this earth just a couple months before *Girls Trip*, so he had missed getting to see how my career took off like a rocket. I would have loved to share that with him, to watch his face crack up at me playing Dina or glow with pride when he saw how much people loved that movie. He missed all of that, and I really missed him.

My dad had talked a lot about his life in Eritrea over the years, but when I went there with his ashes it was my first time in that part of the world. I had visions of a reverse *Coming to America*, where a girl from South Central gets welcomed in Africa as a queen.

When we landed in Asmara, I walked off the plane and breathed in deep. I was standing on the motherland, the real Wakanda, baby. Eritrea has its problems, but this was where my father had spent the first two decades of his life. It was the weirdest thing walking onto that land. My whole soul felt complete. I thought, *Oh wow, this is where I'm supposed to be. I was meant to come here.* The air was so sweet and clean— and ringing through it was this incredible noise: *ELELELE!* All my aunties, my cousins, everyone in my family had gathered there at the airport to greet me, and they were all going "ELELELE!"

I asked a security guard who was leaning against the entrance, "Oh shoot, what's going on? Is there about to be a fight?"

"No, that's a welcome call. They're excited you're here."

ELELELE! Apparently, that's the call you do in Eritrea when you're celebrating, when someone dies, when there's a wedding. It's a call straight from your soul. *ELELELE!* I went to my people to say hello. Let me tell you, it was a trip standing in a circle of people I'd never met before and feeling 100 percent at home. They sounded like me, their faces looked like me, and they were dancing even though there was no music—just like me.

I had been there ten minutes, and I already felt so connected to the history and soul of that country. Everybody should try to go to their roots. Find out where you come from, and go. Even if you don't know nobody, just go. Everyone should know the joy of feeling at home.

My family gave me the red-carpet treatment. My auntie invited me over to her house where they made a feast for me. The food tasted so good, so fresh. The peach tasted like a real peach. Same with the tomatoes and peppers. It was like the best version of each of them. I ate pineapple, which usually makes my mouth itch, and I didn't have an allergic reaction. It was amazing. I must have eaten a lot because after half an hour or so, I needed to use the restroom real bad. My cousins showed me where it was. I hurried with my ass cheeks squeezed to get there so I didn't mess my pants. I wasn't looking around at my surroundings as I ran-walked through the property, which was designed like an Italian villa with a courtyard in the middle. I did my business, and when I came out of the bathroom, I looked over into this small grassy outdoor section of the home between the bathroom and the kitchen. There was blood everywhere, seeping into the red earth.

My first thought was, *Ohmigod, somebody's hurt!* I started yelling, "Somebody's bleeding! Hurry, hurry!" Everyone came running over, and I pointed to all the blood.

My tallest cousin laughed at me and said, "Ohnonono, no one is hurt. We kill goat for you. To welcome you, we kill the goat." No one had ever killed anything for me before.

While I was in Eritrea, I had a guide, a woman named Hanet, to show me around during my visit. Hanet's husband is actually cousin to my cousins. So, kind of like we're cousins, but we're not cousins? Anyways, after a couple days showing me around the country, Hanet said, "You need a pretty dress. You have to go shopping."

We piled into her car, and she took me to these dress shops in town that were full of the most beautiful dresses. I shopped around for a while, running my hand over the shimmering fabrics and imagining how much work each one must have taken to sew.

Then, something took my breath away. This gorgeous dress on a hanger touched my spirit. It had really intricate gold and black embroidery. It came with a crown and two capes. The shorter cape was made of this velvet material, and it was embroidered all over in gold to match the embroidery on the dress. I *loved* it. I took it over to the shopkeeper, and Hanet helped to explain that this was the dress I wanted. They sewed one for me for like sixty bucks. It was too big in the boobs 'cause I got little titties, but it was nothing a safety pin couldn't fix.

That was the dress I pictured myself walking down the red carpet in.

I went to my closet and pulled out my Eritrean dress to show Tiddlywinks. He sort of *mmm mmm*'d and said, "But wait 'til you see the Brandon Maxwell dress. You're probably not going to want to wear this dress. You'll probably want to wear the Brandon Maxwell dress."

"No, I'm pretty much going to wear this dress."

Mind you, even though I liked Tiddlywinks, he was already on thin ice because I had done the cover for *Time* magazine a month or so earlier, and as far as I was concerned, it was a shit show. He'd chosen a high-necked shimmery silver gown with wide bell sleeves and a skirt that looked like a quilt you'd put on your bed in a haunted castle. During the fitting, I kept telling him, "I'm not really feeling this outfit."

"Don't you worry," he said. "It's *high fashion*. You're going to look great." He directed what to do with my makeup and my hair: pink frosted lipstick, lots of eye shadow, super dark eyebrows, crimped wig. I was not loving any of it. But over and over he said, "This is *high fashion*. This is going to be great." So, I let him call the shots.

When that cover came out, it was not *high fashion*. I did not look great. I did not look like Tiffany Haddish. I looked like a goddamn witch, like hocus-motherfucking-pocus. I was about to put a spell on his ass and turn him into a genital wart.

Come Oscar time, this dude was not going to talk me into wearing something I did not want to wear. I was wearing that Eritrean dress for my dad.

The year before he passed away, my dad had come to visit. I was so happy to have him with me. I wanted to give and give to that man to make up for all the years we had spent apart, but he wasn't the best at receiving. At one point, he mentioned he wanted a guitar, so I took him to Guitar Center where we looked at all the guitars.

When he saw the prices, he said, "That's too much. I don't want you spending this kind of money on me. This is too much. This is too much."

I just wanted to buy him a guitar, but he insisted it was too expensive, and I had to honor that.

"Whatever you want, Dad."

We got in my car without a guitar to drive back to my house, and that's when he started telling me if anything were ever to happen to him, it was really important that I wouldn't spend a lot of money to bury him.

"Everyone will be mad, but I want you to cremate me. The tradition is to keep the body whole and to bury me in the ground. But I don't want to cost you money because I've never spent a lot of money on you, so I don't want you spending a lot of money on me. I want to be buried with my mother. But honor me, honor me, and make sure people know about our people, that the world knows about Eritrea. If you become a big star, when you have a big moment, you have to represent your ancestors. My mother was a star in Eritrea—you have to represent her. You have to represent me, my father, our heritage. Nobody knows about us. You must make sure the world knows."

I thought, *How am I gonna do that? Nobody knows about me. I'm just on a TV show. People barely know I exist.* But I told him I would. I would do anything he wanted me to do.

It felt totally out of the blue at the time, but now that I look back, I realize he must have already known he was near the end of his life.

For the last few months of his life, my father kept talking about how he wanted to go to Eritrea with me someday to take me to his homeland. It was like he had to get this wish out there in the world before he left it. He said, "I want to be able to take you. I don't have the money yet, but when I get the money, I'm gonna take you."

He died before he could take me, but I was glad I was able to honor his wishes by taking his ashes to Eritrea. I wanted to honor his other wish, too, to bring attention to Eritrea.

He had not said, "Go fight a war for Eritrea." He hadn't said, "Give all your money to Eritrea," or "Make sure that the country's built up good." He'd said, "Make sure people know that Eritrea exists." So, I was planning to wear a traditional Eritrean dress to one of the largest events in the world, the Oscars, no matter what my stylist had planned. But my stylist was not getting the fucking message.

Once it became clear to him that I wasn't just running my mouth, I was serious, Tiddlywinks called everyone on my team—my representation, my publicist, my hair and makeup (Everyone but my gynecologist) to try to convince me not to wear the Eritrean dress.

They did not have my back. Everyone said, "Look, Tiffany, everyone wears known designers. Just wear the Brandon Maxwell."

That was some shit. How were they gonna tell me not to honor my dead dad's wish? I cried a billion tears because I felt like no one would approve of me wearing my beautiful African dress. But *I* fucking approved. Not everybody's going to like everything I do. But I knew what I wanted to stand for. I knew what I was representing. I was done letting people tell me what to wear. I'd already earned my Big Tiff Energy. I knew who I was. Once you know that and then somebody's trying to change you and make you be something you're not, it is the most uncomfortable, horrible feeling in the world. Do *not* try to tell me how to look or who to be.

I was going to go with what I wanted to wear. I was dressing for me, for my daddy, my people. I'd made up my mind. And I told them, "On the red carpet, I'm going to wear my Eritrean dress. When I get onstage to present, I'm going to wear my Alexander McQueen dress. And then when I go to the parties, I'll wear the Brandon Maxwell dress and that's what it's going to be."

Even then, folks were saying, "You're taking a big chance. You need to be prepared not to get good press." I was fine with that. As long as they talked about Eritrea, I was fine with it.

The week before the show, I tried on the Brandon Maxwell dress my stylist had arranged for me. It was lime green with a strap on one shoulder. The other shoulder was bare. Then it went straight down to the floor with a slit on one side, so I was showing some leg, and there was a little train on the back. I looked at myself in that dress, tailored like I had been born in it, and I had to admit it was stunning. But I said, "This is gorgeous. I love the dress, but nothing has changed for me. I'm still wearing the Eritrean dress."

The day of the Oscars, I woke up in my hotel room, heart skipping along and a happy glow in my cheeks. Big day. Big moment. For an important awards show like the Oscars, you start prepping hours and hours before the event. Tiddlywinks was the first one to show up to get me ready. Soon as he walked in the door, I said, "Okay, where's my dress?" He handed me the Brandon Maxwell and said, "You're wearing this."

I got real calm and let out a little laugh. You know it's dangerous when a woman's upset about something and she starts giggling.

"No, I'm wearing my Eritrean dress."

I am from South Central, so you can only push me so far before I snap. And Tiddlywinks knew this, but that didn't stop him. He held out the Brandon Maxwell. "No, you're wearing *this*. You need to wear this, Tiffany. Just trust me. I know better."

"No, you don't know better. Where's my dress?"

Turns out, *he didn't even bring the dress*. I could not have been clearer about my feelings and my intentions. Had someone erased this dude's memory with one of those space sticks from *Men in Black*?

Let me tell you what I felt then. A few years ago, I found out that someone had taken the money out of my piggy bank right out my closet where I'd hid it. They had only left one cent or two cents in there. When I discovered that, I felt so violated I wanted to beat some ass.

When that stylist came into that room without my dress, I felt like I caught somebody trying to rob me. My wishes were being disrespected. I was being violated. My hood instincts kicked in. You fuck with my shit, my money, my vision—you try to destroy my soul? I'm gonna come at you.

When I'm about to fight, it's funny because the first thing I do is I smile. Then, my eyes dart everywhere because I'm looking to see

Where do I swing? I looked at my stylist, my heart pounding hard. I got instant abs, right tight. I felt very strong in my arms, very strong in my core, very stable in my feet. Grounded, but light, like I was Billy Blanks. Then the smile slowly went away, and it was *Let's go, motherfucker.*

All reason left my body, and all that was left was pure emotion. I wanted to make this guy hurt the way I hurt. I started twitching real bad. I envisioned myself jumping over the bed and punching Tiddlywinks in the head. In my mind, I gave him some Laura Croft shit and busted him in the face like he was a demon in a tomb. *Pa-pow!*

But I took a deep breath, because I was thirty-eight years old, and I knew better. I shouldn't be hitting people. So, I started shooting words.

"Listen up, motherfucker. Where's my dress?"

"It's still with the seamstress."

"Oh, it's not here? It's with the seamstress? When the dress going to get here, then? What time are you bringing it?"

I knew I shouldn't have—it was not very professional—but I got very immature very fast. I used words like "dookie breath" and "doo-doo head." I got very aggressive. It feels good to let it rip when you have that righteous anger going. There's joy letting the hurt out.

I had worked my way from doing stand-up in small clubs to going to the fucking Oscars. I was living what my dad had predicted for me. That was a real moment, and I was not feeling a different dress. When I'm not feeling something, it always turns out bad. Always. I can feel it in my whole body. It's like all my organs shut down. Everything is broken. Nothing works. My kidneys say, "Nope. We're tired." My liver's like, "I know I have three hundred functions I'm supposed to be doing. I'm only going to do ten." My root chakra puts up a sign that says, "Closed for business." The worst part is my soul is like, "Nah, bitch, this not happening. I'm out." I was not about to walk out on a red carpet with millions of people watching without my soul. I don't function well without my soul. My soul is like a whole 'nother person inside me with her own ideas of what we should be about. If I walk into a situation I shouldn't be at or I do something I shouldn't be doing, my soul says, "Peace. I'll be back with you when you finish this dumb shit." I try to call her: "Come back. Come here, girl. Come on. I need you." But she's gone.

I knew if I didn't wear my dress, it was going to be a bad night. My soul would not have showed up. My soul would have been sitting in the car smoking weed while she waited for me to do what I had to do without her, saying, "No. Nuh-uh. I ain't fucking with you over there. That's the devil. I'm over here with God. I'm with the angels. Holla at me when you good." The night would've been horrible.

I told my stylist, "Ain't no way in hell I'm going anywhere 'til you get my dress. Go get my fucking Eritrean princess dress."

Three hours later, he comes in with the dress and a funky little attitude. I put it on and saw it had not been taken in. No alterations had happened whatsoever. I guess Tiddlywinks had figured, "If there ain't no alterations to it, she ain't going to wear it." Uh-uh. I put that bitch on. It was not a perfect fit, but it was just fucking right. My soul was like, "That's what's up. Let's go."

Cut to the red carpet. I strolled down that motherfucker like I was the queen of the world. Cameras snapped a thousand times a minute, everyone going, "Tiffany, over here!" At one point, I hitched up my skirt and jumped over the velvet rope to bow down to my godmother Meryl Streep. Every time I stopped, all the interviewers asked me, "Who are you wearing?" I stood up tall. "My father was Eritrean. He died this past year, and he told me if I ever made it big, I should honor my people, so I'm wearing an Eritrean dress, and I'm proud of it." My soul was like, "Yeah, girl, glad you showed up. Good for you. You made your daddy proud."

When I finished the carpet, all these people told me I looked beautiful. I *felt* beautiful. I went on Twitter, and there were thousands and thousands of tweets saying, "That's right. She's our Eritrean princess." "She's the queen." So many people chimed in super nice remarks. But the best thing was that people were asking, "What is Eritrea? Where is that?" People were googling Eritrea.

I got back to my hotel to change dresses before I went to the parties. My hair and makeup people were there and they said, "You did so good. That was so beautiful. You looked amazing."

I *felt* beautiful. I *felt* amazing. Everything lined up that night like planets during an eclipse—success, my love for my dad, me standing up for what I wanted, my dope-ass dress. It was the perfect conditions for joy.

My stylist came in, all sheepish, and I had no more harsh words for him. "I guess I was wrong," he said. "I guess you do know what you're talking about."

That's right, I do. Ain't nobody gonna tell me different. *ELELELE!*

HEY LADIES

I AM A CHAMP at giving advice. If you want suggestions for how to clear up your sinuses, I will help you out. You want to know where to get the best tacos in LA, hit me up. You have a question about your finances, I will break it down for you. But the one thing I will not tell you how to do is choose a husband. That is not an area of expertise for me. However, if you are just looking for a good time, I *got* you. I have been sexual with forty-eight dudes in my life. I know the exact number because I keep track of any sexual activity where juices were present in a notebook I keep tucked up inside my vagina in a Ziploc baggie. Mouth fucking and finger banging count, but dry humping does not. I write down the guy's first name, the first letter of his last name, a little blurb about him, and a note about what I called his dick—Mr. Wiggly, Waldo (like, where is he?), Daddy D., or Tyrone if he's super big (haven't had one of those in a minute). Through those experiences, I have learned a thing or two about how to be with a man in the physical sense. This might sound like some ratchet shit, but I'm a comedian and that comes with the territory, so here go Tiff's tips for a happy and healthy sex life.

Make Sure He Is Mr. Clean

The first thing you need to know if you want to be fucking is that if a man's house is dirty, nasty, and run down, and if his body is not squeaky clean, you should walk away. Turn your ass around, and go eat some beef jerky. If you're still horny, get yourself some battery-powered action instead. Just do not get naked with him if he's raggedy because if he doesn't value his property or himself, he sure as hell isn't going to value you.

I'm a firm believer that every time you sleep with someone, they take a little piece of your soul with them, and you keep a little piece of theirs with you. You sleep with mean motherfuckers who don't value you, you carry that with you. You gave up a little piece of yourself to someone who didn't deserve it. I'd rather give a little piece of myself to someone who appreciates a good thing.

That's why I like a man who smells like soap; when you hug him, a little puff of laundry detergent scent comes off. Nice moisturized skin. Hair trimmed up. Clothes that came from a dresser or out of a closet, not off a pile on the floor. Shoes should not be all worn down on the soles, no scuffs. Tidy.

I like to inspect the whole package when it shows up at my door before I tear it open . . . starting with the hands.

You know that joke they say about a man with big feet? Well, it ain't actually about the feet. If you want to know what he has going on downstairs, check his hands. If his hands are dry and ashy, his dick is probably ashy, too. My grandma used to say, "Dirty nails, dirty D. Keep that thing away from me."

I've done research, so I know that is true. When I was younger, anytime I would go out on a date, first thing I would do when we got back to my place was ask if I could see his penis. (Men, as a reminder, *only if she asks*.) I would pull out my disposable camera and say, "Can I take a picture of it? I don't need your face or anything. I just want to remember your penis." Most guys were happy to whip it out. They'd be holding it in their hands, and sure enough you could see the tip of the penis usually matched the fingernails. Dirty nails, dirty dick. If you meet a man who does not have clean hands, either send him packing or make sure he takes a nice long time in the shower before you let him in your underpants. Just don't let him slather a bunch of lotions and potions on his dick. You don't want to mess up your pH balance.

I don't mind jacked-up teeth. They can be on top of each other or far apart from each other or really little. Doesn't matter. Your teeth can look like a rabbit's, and I will still mess with you as long as you are keeping up good dental hygiene. It makes me nauseous when a guy's breath smells like old milk and he's trying to kiss me. I will grab a lemon and tell him, "I think you have a dead tooth. I can smell it from over here. I want to fuck you, but if I let you go down on me, I'm afraid I'm going to get bacterial vaginosis. You need to brush your teeth and then eat this lemon."

The first time I got bacterial vaginosis, I thought my uterus was dead 'cause it smelled so bad. You do not need a dead skunk in your baby oven, so make sure he brushes and flosses before you do it.

Blowjobs Are Important

Next, if you want a man to be sweating, you better suck it until you get the wrinkles out of his balls. I learned that from my grandma.

That's right. From my grandma. When I was in my twenties, I was over at my grandma's house visiting her. I was looking through some magazines on the couch when she crossed the living room to sit beside me. I smelled her dried flower smell as she wrapped her soft, old lady fingers around my forearm and gave it a little squeeze. I could tell from the face she was making that she was about to offer me some wise words.

She cleared her throat a little and said, "Baby girl, let me tell you something. If you trying to keep your man at home, because you know men like to wander, there is one thing you've got to learn how to do."

I thought she might tell me that I needed to have dinner on the table every night or put some lipstick on once in a while.

"Grandma, what you talking about?"

"Tiffany, child." She waved her finger at me like a schoolteacher. "You gonna have to kiss that banana every day."

My eyes bugged out of my head. What did she just say? My grandmother was a proper lady—you might even say prissy—who wore her blouses buttoned all the way up to the throat and went to services every week. She had given me all kinds of advice but never about slurping on it.

Now, I was not opposed to giving a BJ. I had already sucked the occasional dick by that point in my life because the girls I went to high school with in that white neighborhood used to tell me, "You want your man to get you a new Honda? You got to make sure he is dehydrated." I was taking the bus everywhere back then, and a new Civic sounded pretty good to me. So, I had given it a try, but I had not become a specialist or anything. I just sort of licked the ice cream cone a couple of times—*mmmm, mmmm, you're welcome*—and called it a night. I never did get a Honda. But now here was my grandma in her purple church dress sitting next to me and telling me I needed to choke on it if I wanted to keep my man.

To be real, my grandma had five kids by four baby daddies, so you know she was a killer in bed. She was getting it on in the 1950s and 1960s when folks were really fucking. Later in life, she became a Jehovah's Witness because she realized she might have been a ho, but even if those days were behind her, she obviously still had some opinions about how to make a man happy.

I said, "Ewwwww. That's nasty, Grandma. What if he isn't even washing that banana every day?"

She patted my arm. "Baby girl, it may be nasty, but you listen to me. If you do that, you won't be lonely."

My grandma was right. Sucking dick is the secret to a banging sex life. When I see a couple that's been together twenty years still glowing, I know she's been giving head. Especially if they only have one or two kids. That tells me she's been swallowing that baby batter or letting it hit her face instead of getting her pregnant. That's why her skin looks so good because sperm is good for you.

I ran my own study on that, too. When I was bald on the sides because my edges were gone from too many hair weaves, I got a man, yanked him off, took that sperm, and rubbed it across my hairline. My hair grew back thick and beautiful 'cause my hair follicles were pregnant with protein. Whenever I see a bald-headed man, I want to tell him he should go jack off in his hands and rub that sperm on his bald spot. See if that hair don't grow back.

But back to blowjobs. Straight men don't realize how hard it is to suck dick every fucking day. It's a lot of work on your jaws. When a man eats my coochie, all I need him to do is put his face down there and go *ppbbbbbb, mamasaymamasahmamakusa*. Sucking dick takes energy and effort. You've got to have hand-eye coordination. You've got to watch your teeth, keep the rhythm. It's a whole thing. When I have been pleasing a man on a regular basis, I get carpal tunnel in my throat, my sciatica gets all fucked up, and I need a heating pad for my neck. But Granny said you can't be a punk about it, so I keep my mouth skills on point.

My technique for giving head is to wrap my lips around that thang and cough a little bit when he hits my throat (even if he's real small) so I can make him feel like he's a big man. Then I get noisy, making smacking sounds and going *mmm, ahhh, eh, eh*. That drives 'em wild.

When he's ready to pop, I look him in the eye like I'm blessing him. That pushes him right over the edge.

A blowjob is a beautiful thing if you are doing it right. Here's how you can tell if you are doing a good job:

1. He's gonna cuss—"Oh god, oh my fucking god, shit, baby, that feels so good. I'm gonna buy you a mother-fucking Corvette"—even if he's a rabbi. I know that from experience.

2. His face gets so twisted he looks like he lost a chromo-some. His eyes go way back in his head so he's looking at the front of his brain. His mouth opens like a fish on the dock gasping for air—*pwop, pwop, pwop*—right before he hits that high-pitched "Oh shiiiiiiiiiiiiiiiiiit."

3. When he finally busts a nut, he bucks like he got shot in the chest. He looks like he's dying slowly and you're resuscitating him by those electric paddles.

You get your man to do those three things, and I promise you he is sticking around to make you biscuits in the morning.

But You Don't Have to Suck as Much D as You Think You Do

Using your mouth isn't as important as using your ears. I learned that at the worst job I ever had: phone sex operator. I didn't know I was even applying for the job when I got it. I had just graduated from high school, and I needed some money. I didn't have anybody else to pay my rent, or to pay for me to get my hair done, get my nails done, or pay my phone bill. That was all on me.

Me and my best friend searched the classifieds in the back of the *Backstage West* magazine. All the acting jobs asked for headshots and resumes, which seemed like it would require a lot of trips to Kinko's and the post office, so we passed on those. But then we found an ad that said they were looking for voice actors. We were like, "We got voices!" So, we got in her Nissan Altima and went to the address listed, which took us to this generic office building right on Sunset.

We parked and got in the elevator up to the third floor. *Bing.* Out we went into a corporate, clean-cut lobby space. Everything was squared off. No decorations except a fake plant in the corner. It could have been a doctor's office or maybe a therapist's.

We walked up to the front reception desk. It was raised up off the ground in sort of a booth, like at the police station. First thing I noticed about the girl behind the desk was she had a tattoo on her neck. This was in '98. There were not a lot of neck tattoos at that time. If you had a name on your neck back then, you were a killer. Killa had a little attitude, too. She gave me and my friend one of those little head tilt, raised eyebrow looks as we approached.

"How may I help you?"

I smiled big. "Yeah, we're here for the job interview."

Killa picked up the phone real slow like she was doing us a favor and called somebody.

After a minute or two, a busted Scott Baio–looking dude in khaki pants came over and gestured for us to sit down in two chairs near the front of the booth.

He cleared his throat. "You guys are here to be voice actors?"

We nodded. Killa sniffed like something was funny to her. We ignored her and focused on what this man was saying.

"Okay, before we get started, I need you to know this is an eighteen-and-over job." He looked us over close like maybe we had just shoplifted something. "How old are you guys anyway?" We showed him our IDs. After he checked them, he nodded and handed us a couple of loose pieces of paper.

"I'm going to need you to read this to me."

I looked down at the first line. "Hi, my name is [name]. What's your name? What do you do, caller?"

Charles in Charge tapped his pen against his leg for a second in case we hadn't put the pieces together before he explained, "This is a phone sex operator line."

I looked at my homegirl. Both of our eyes were big as hell. This was not what I'd had in mind. I'd pictured us reading lines for Palmolive commercials, not talking dirty to dirty old men. But I really wanted that check. I'd been emancipated from my family, and I needed to pull together money for a place to live. I was going to do what I had to do. Khaki pants kept talking. Eventually, my bestie and I just looked at each other and shrugged like, "Well, that makes sense," because it was a lot of money they were promising per hour.

We each read the script out loud, but not even in a sexy way—just like we were reading instructions to a board game or something. Apparently, that was good enough for him.

"Okay. Go sit in booth five."

We walked back to a grid of cubicles where about thirty women and, I was surprised to see, a few men wore headsets like they were sports commentators. That first day, they had us sit next to somebody to watch them work for two hours before we started making calls on our own. Like a buddy system.

We went over to booth five where they had set us up with a thirty-something woman named Karla. She had those dark skinny eyebrows, lips lined, and hair that flipped back with the little bangs that went forward. When she stood up to shake hands, her skirt was holding on for dear life. She was wearing clothes from those boutiques that have mannequins on the sidewalk out front with cute little outfits on them, but the fabric is so cheap that when you put it on a real body, it squeezes you like a sausage and gives you a muffin top.

Karla explained there were a bunch of different lines people could call—two girls and one guy, MILFs, that kind of thing. Certain lines had different rules. We started out on the ninety-nine-cents-a-minute line where you're not allowed to cuss. You're not allowed to say any words that people commonly use for penis, vagina, or breasts. You have to talk in code. It was like an X-rated game of Password. If you said the wrong word on that line, then you got docked three dollars. I needed that money, so I was not about to slip.

Karla was hella good at the job. Between her calls, she pressed her finger on the desk and gave us tips and pointers.

"Dudes want you to talk dirty, but you know you can't so you have to get creative. If he goes, 'What are you doing now?' you say, 'Oh, I'm just in here playing with my toys.' Then you take your pager and put it right next to the speaker of the phone and make it vibrate on the table." Instant vibrator noise.

She told me I had to come up with a fantasy persona for the caller to imagine on the other end of the line. I decided my persona was going to be named Patricia.

When it was my turn to answer a call, I'd pick up the line and say, "Hi, caller. My name is Patricia. I'm five-six, I am Black and Hawaiian, I grew up in Hawaii, and I have long black hair that kisses my booty when I walk. I'm a 36DD. And I'm a cheerleader at USC."

Doing phone sex for money taught me that men are into some weird shit. There was one dude with a real deep voice who wanted to hear about my feet all the time. He'd call me up sounding like Barry White.

"Hey, Patricia, I can't get enough of your corns, babe. How about you send me a picture of those bunions?"

I was like *nah*, but I did consider sending him a photo of my grandma's feet. They were old and scaly like she mixed with alligators. I'm sure he would have had a good old time with that picture.

I was curious about the men who worked the lines. Sometimes they talked in a fake girl voice, and sometimes they just used their normal speaking voices. Over the next couple weeks, I noticed these men made more money than any of the women operators. One day, I sat next to one of them, and I figured out why. This guy knew how to talk to other men, how to keep them on the line while the dollars racked up. He talked about sports, politics, and the weather and would just be silly with them. *Tick, tick, tick, ka-ching.* The other thing I noticed was he would go for a long time being really quiet, just listening to the caller.

That's when it clicked for me: these callers weren't just nasty; they were *lonely.* They wanted someone to talk to just as much as they wanted to get off. I started talking less and listening more. If I let them, dudes on the other end of my line would be vulnerable, sweet, and sensitive.

Some of them poured their hearts out to me. They just wanted to feel like someone gave a shit about what happened to them each day. Like if one of their coworkers said something to them that they didn't like, they'd hold that inside them all day long 'til eleven o'clock at night when they would call me and say, "Patricia, are you there? Hi, baby. I have to tell you about something. My boss doesn't appreciate me. I busted my balls getting her this analysis, and all she said was, 'Just put it on my desk.' My wife never listens to me when I try to talk to her. She's always running off to her kickboxing class or some shit." They'd go on like that for a while and then start talking about their mom. They were basically paying me to say, "And then what happened, baby?"

Fifteen minutes later, they'd be like, "Oh shoot! I forgot I was supposed to be touching my penis!"

After I had had a couple of calls with a guy, 90 percent of the time, they would let out a big sigh and say, "You're the only one I can talk to, Patricia."

"How can that be true? You are such a good guy. I bet you're very handsome."

"You really think so?" I could hear the hope perk up through their voice, like maybe they were worth paying attention to after all.

It was that simple.

I only lasted thirty days at that job. For every man who was on the line for some company, there were ten who were just nasty. I could only have so many discussions about what a dude wanted to do with a hairbrush and some Chapstick before it started eating at my soul, but the experience taught me sometimes you just have to let him know you are as willing to receive his words as you are his sperm.

Show Him a Good Time—Yours

Finally, and this is probably the most important thing I will say to you about sex, I do not want to hear that you are leaving your bedroom unsatisfied. It is the twenty-first century, girl. If he has fun, you have to have fun, too. I'm not just talking about coming, though that definitely needs to happen if you want it to. I'm talking about an all-over satisfaction. When you're rubbing uglies, you need to let your man know you want him to provoke joy that's going to radiate up through your spirit.

You should enjoy yourself when you are smashing. He should be making you feel beautiful and sexy. Don't spend all your time trying to guess what's inside his head, going, "Does he like this?" or "Ouch, his beard is scratching me, but if I say something he's going to think I'm not grateful. It'll be over in a minute anyway." That is bullshit. There is a lot of good dick out there attached to good men. Most men want you to be happy. If you are not getting what you need, ask for it. A closed mouth doesn't get fed.

Good men love to see light; they love to see you smile. True, from-the-heart joy is a turn-on. If your man thinks it will make you giggle, he'll do the silliest shit in bed. He'll pretend to be Tickle Me Elmo or slap his D from thigh to thigh just to make you laugh. He won't be offended because you're laughing. He'll be thinking he's the king because he made you feel so good. Remember this—if you let him know you're laughing during sex 'cause it feels so good inside your spirit, he's gonna try to be inside of you all the time.

And do not play dumb to get a man to like you. I see that nonsense all the time—a girl will act stupid so a dude won't feel intimidated. Smarts make a guy's D hard. Intelligent men, that's their thing. They get off on a woman who knows her mind. Any time you feel like you have to change yourself—your ideas or how you talk or act or what your body looks like—to be with a man, that's already a problem. He should want you to feel good in his presence, not like you have to hide your light. You are perfect the way God made you. Let that man celebrate God's creation. Let him worship your ass. Let him get down on his knees and praise what the good Lord has made. Just be sure he brushed his teeth first.

HOW I KEEP MY ASS IN CHECK

JUST ABOUT EVERY INTERVIEW I have ever done, the host has asked me some version of "You have not had it easy, girl. How come you so positive all the time?"

I would love to say that I am a magical unicorn who has been blessed with an abundance of mental health, but the real answer is *it is work*.

I sucked my thumb every single day of my life until I was eighteen years old. Just like a baby. Anytime I felt a full mess, I popped my thumb in my mouth, *mwah, mwah, mwah*. A *self-soother*, they call it. It's a miracle I never had to wear braces, but I did used to have strep throat like a motherfucker.

I don't suck my thumb anymore, but I do take other actions to keep this brain in check.

My life is in a good place on paper. I know that. I did a TV show in 2021 where I made more money per episode than I thought I'd ever see in my life. I own a home in Los Angeles, and I can pay my mortgage on time. I'm a goddamn A-list celebrity. But I'm not indestructible. My confidence goes up and down like anyone else 'cause I got hormones. There are days where I wonder, *Why am I on this planet again?* Other times, I will be on social media and see people on there saying the meanest things about me. It is hard enough to feel good about yourself, but when every fucking thing you do gets blasted across the internet, it can feel impossible.

Somewhere out there, there's video footage of me at the Laugh Factory, telling the audience that they should do at least one thing for themselves every day.

"If you can do at least one thing for yourself," I tell them. "Just one thing that makes you feel better, life will be a little more joyful. You do things for yourself to remember that what you need matters."

That's damn good advice. I wish I could take it.

There was one especially hard time in my life when I had just lost someone important, three someones actually, but the most important one was my grandma. She had raised me and now she was gone. Growing up, I felt like I was constantly losing people, so now when I lose people I care about, my primal brain goes, *Hope you like being alone! You're not going to have anybody. When you die, they're going to find your corpse in your apartment and your cat looking guilty.* When I got the call, I got so panicky. It felt like my heart was gasping for air. What I needed was time to grieve, but because I do not want everyone thinking I am an evil, mean bitch who doesn't do her job, I did the minimum for me and the maximum for everyone else. I was on a shoot, but I flew across the country, paid my respects, and then flew immediately back across the country for my 6:00 a.m. call time. I did twenty-seven interviews that day. I tried to hold it together, be professional, but sometimes my feelings came out of my face. It worked all right for the interviewers—they just used all the funny parts and cut all the parts of me crying—but it didn't work for me. I was barely human by the end of that day. I should have listened to my own advice and taken care of myself.

When I don't take care of me, that's when I make mistakes. It never fails. When I neglect me and put myself last, that's when I let other people and myself down. The way I see it, my mistakes are like warning signs from the universe to get my shit together and start taking care of myself already. I try to go, *Okay, universe, you right. I been slacking. I've been kind of lightweight hatin' on me. I'm so busy trying to do stuff for other people and make things grow around me that I'm taking away from myself. Time to fix that.*

Here's what I do to get back to Tiffany: 1) I do some work on myself inside and out. I get myself to therapy, eat raw food, kick that smoke and drink for a while, get some rest. 2) I try to talk myself into asking for help. Asking for help doesn't exactly come naturally because I'm so used to having to take care of myself, but I'm working on it. It's scary. When I go, "Hey, guys? I could use some support right now," and it's crickets? *Pffff,* that's a whole level of feeling alone and worthless, and I start thinking about my body in my apartment again. But I know there are people out there who will actually listen to what I have to say. There are people that really, really love me, and as much as I hate asking, I can count on them. And 3) I make time to do everyday, human things. I walk my own dog, wash my own clothes, and water my own plants to remind me that even though I live in the public eye, I am a regular person with a regular person body that needs rest and a regular person heart that needs love.

None of that makes me perfect. I'm not saying that. But I am learning how to deal with my problems. Will I forget to take care of myself and make another mistake? I certainly hope not. But I know one mistake I will never make is not learning from my mistakes.

Whenever I'm going through some tumultuous shit, whether it's dealing with haters online or a project falling through or a relationship exploding, here's my secret: I say to myself, "Hold on, Tiff, let's take a look at what you've been doing. How are *you* treating you? What kind of communication are you having with yourself? Are you saying that you are stupid? That you worthless? That you got a lazy eye?"

Every time I'm in the dumps in my life, it's because I've invited bad energy with the way I've talked shit about myself. Maybe I don't remember doing it. Maybe I don't remember saying to myself, "You can't do this," or "You're not good at that." But then three days later, a week later, a month later, that shit manifests. That bad energy perpetuates more negativity, more hurt, and less confidence, which leads to less of an ability to create the things I want to create. I go, "Oh, man, I keep fucking up. I am a fuckup. Yep, there I go again, fucking up." And then before I know it, everything's fucked up.

My emotions are my compass, the energy that guides and leads me. So, if I give that negative thought a lot of energy, a lot of feeling, that's going to be a bad situation. I have to counteract that.

So, what I do is I take those automatic negative thoughts—therapists call them ANTS—out of the conversation with myself. I kill those destructive little fuckers. I'm like, "Shut up, ANTS! Stop it!" I crush them, stomp 'em out. I annihilate them, grind 'em under my heel into nasty little ant paste to make room for better thoughts.

I go to the mirror. I look at the little black part of my eye and stare at myself there, just that part. I don't look at the rest of my head, my clothes, nothing. Just the pupil. I say my full name, *Tiffany Sarah Cornelia Haddish*, and then I tell myself, "I love and approve of you." I do that for five minutes—*Tiffany Sarah Cornelia Haddish, I love and approve of you. Tiffany Sarah Cornelia Haddish, I love and approve of you*—and then my confidence level is *on*. My joy starts bubbling right back up. I learned this from the writer Louise Hay and it helped me so much. The first time I did it, I didn't even last a minute. I got through maybe thirty seconds before I had to stop 'cause I didn't feel that way about myself. But then, the more I did it, the more my life changed for the better.

I will look into my eyeballs and tell myself how fucking awesome I am. I speak to all the cells that live in me: *Look at you, you little atoms and neutrons. I'm proud of you. You doing a great job. You're splitting, growing, healing. Look at you, liver—you handled last night well. I'm sorry I made you work so hard. You're doing a great job of getting that poison out.*

I tell myself, "You got this, girl. You got the divine energy spread all over you. Pull that energy from your uterus." I charge myself up. Nobody gets to control my emotions but me.

The words you say are like magic making things happen in the world. When you give yourself love, when you say, "Self, you are the shit. Look at you. You're smart, you're funny, you're a great dancer. The world is so lucky to have you," your subconscious is like, "Oh, she think she great? I better get out there and build a world worthy of this person." You can't rely on other people to give you joy. You have to practice giving joy to yourself. Curse *yourself* with joy.

I don't know. It works for me. Try it. See if you can manifest some self-love. Maybe some good things for yourself. If not, you always got your thumb.

O, NICOLAS CAGE

BACK WHEN I WAS seventeen, I went to see the movie *Face/Off* at the Hawthorne Theatre. That is a great movie, though it is proof that white people can get damn near anything made.

I can just imagine the pitch—*Nicolas Cage, John Travolta, dead son, face transplant.* I bet they sold it in the room.

It was the perfect date movie. It had thrills and chills, but it was not full of oogie-boogies that would haunt my dreams.

I saw it with my first real boyfriend, Jerry. He took me to the last showing of the night. We got our popcorn and walked into the dark theatre.

Even though there were like six other people in the theatre and we could have sat right in the middle, Jerry said, "Yo, let's sit back here."

He walked way back to the very last row. I had worn a cute skirt, but it was short as fuck. I had to tug it down so it would cover my booty when I sat.

About halfway through the movie, Jerry leaned in and gave me a licky-lick behind my ear. You ever had anyone do that? It'll make your baby hairs stand on end. Nipples, too. It was *very* distracting, but in a good way. It was my first time making out in a movie theatre, but I guessed it wasn't Jerry's. He knew last row was make-out row. We started kissing, and then we really got into it. His hands were everywhere—on my face, in my hair, on my thighs. He went for a little titty action, and then he crept his fingers up my skirt. *Hello.* He started fiddling about. I had not been fiddled with before—and I liked it. A lot.

I felt a weird pressure down there where he was touching me—a good pressure, like someone tickling my insides right by my bladder. That feeling . . . whoa, it was crazy. It did something to how I was breathing. I started panting like a dog on a summer day. *Heh heh heh heh.* The pressure kept building, but I didn't want to stop it. It got to where I thought I was going to pee on myself. *I'm going to ruin my skirt. Should I put a stop to this? Nah. Fuck it.* The skirt would dry.

I closed my eyes and gave myself over to the pressure. Just as things were about to go off, I opened my lids and there was Nicolas Cage on-screen. His piercing blue eyes were looking into my soul as I was achieving a momentous moment for the first time in my life. I'm sure we watched to the end of the movie, but the action on-screen definitely took a back seat to the action in my pants. Jerry and I stayed together for another year or so after that, and I popped off more than a few times while he was fiddling the bean. Our relationship fizzled out, but I was always grateful to him for my first orgasm. And I always felt a little something-something anytime I saw Nicolas Cage's eyes on-screen.

Flash-forward twenty years. I'm in Budapest filming a movie called *The Unbearable Weight of Massive Talent.* Nicolas Cage is the lead. So now I am staring into those very same eyes in *real actual life* that had been looking at me the first time I came.

Now, I had been super excited about working with Nicolas Cage because he is an amazing actor. Just mind-blowing. *Leaving Las Vegas, Raising Arizona, National Treasure*—I was raised on those movies. But this was the first time I had met him in person.

Dude has been making movies since I was a one-year-old. I could only imagine the stories he could tell.

When I'd come into the room where we were going to be filming—a pretty simple set with just a chair and a desk—in walked Cage in a pink leather jacket. Looked like bubble gum with all these patches stuck to it—an elephant, a gun, the Superman S, angel's wings. I had heard that he liked to wear leather jackets, especially the first time he met someone. Maybe to intimidate people? I don't know what the tea was with that. He had on a mask 'cause of COVID, so all I could really see of his face were his eyes.

Oh lordy. Those eyes.

It was a busy room. The director, the AD, the grips, boom operator, hair, and makeup were buzzing around focused on their tasks—getting lights in place and checking the sound—so I do not think a single person there noticed how I was locked in on Nicolas Cage's eyes.

Once we were both ready to start rehearsing, it was on. Mr. Nicolas Cage was not about a lot of foreplay/getting-to-know-you warm-up chitchat. It was, "Nice to meet you. Let's do this scene. Here's how it's going to go. Okay? Okay. Good, let's run it through."

I had prepared. I knew all my lines, all my marks. I knew everything, but the hardest thing for me is when I don't know the person I'm in a scene with because I do not know what they are going to bring out in me.

What Nic Cage brought out was the memory of my first Big O. There was a movie running in my head, but it was not the one we were filming.

Nic delivered his lines like a pro and then gave me space. But I just stared at those blue eyes like I was hypnotized. I tried to talk, activate my vocal cords, but no words came out. I just moved my mouth without any sound. I was having a *Face/Off* moment in my brain. *Holy shit. What is happening? Why am I seventeen years old again? If I peeled off Nic Cage's face, would the dude who gave me that whoa feeling be under there?* Not an optimal mindset for rehearsing with one of the world's biggest movie stars. I was fucking up. *Tiffany Haddish, you are a way better performer than this. Ohmigod, they're paying you all this money and you suck. Get it together, girl.*

BRAIN: Do you remember that day?

ME: Of course I remember that day. You know what they say. You never forget your first.

BRAIN: His blue eyes were looking at you like they are right now. You got very moist and then you were all, "Ughaaaaah." Remember?

ME: I said I remembered. Damn. Aren't you in charge of memories?

BRAIN: Just tell him that story so this can go away.

Cage looked up at the sky, like, "Any day now, Haddish."
"What's the problem, Tiffany?" He was getting irritated.
I told him, "Listen, I want to do this, but I'm intimidated."
"Tiffany Haddish, intimidated?"

BRAIN: JUST TELL HIM.

The crew did not say a word. They just kept setting up C stands and stuff for when the cameras were going to roll as if I weren't freaking out in the middle of the set.

"Look, I have to tell you this story. It's very inappropriate, and I probably shouldn't tell it, but there is no way I'm going to make it through this day if I don't get this off my spirit right now. I have to tell you, man."

Cage tucked his thumbs in his pockets and nodded. "Go ahead and tell me."

"Are you sure? I don't want you to sue me or say I'm harassing you."

He raised his eyebrows like, "Please do not make me say 'tell me' again."

So, I told him all about how I got off at *Face/Off.*

"And now every time you look at me in my eyes you make me think of that guy. I keep seeing him in my head. This is why I am having a problem saying my lines."

Ahhhhhhhh. There. I'd said it. I was either going to be able to do this job now or I was going to be fired.

Nicolas Cage's eyes crinkled way up as he cracked up laughing. "That's crazy. That's a crazy story." He caught his breath. "Let me tell *you* something now. Before we were married, my first wife was on a date and she saw a movie with me in it and she told the guy, 'I'm going to marry him.' And we did actually get married. Crazy."

Now you hold on there, Nicolas Cage.

I just wanted to get that off my chest so I could get back to doing my job. I'm not saying I want to marry you or that I need you touching me. But we will be looking into each other's eyes, so let's get to it.

It was like I'd sneezed . . . or masturbated. Once I got that memory out, it was a reboot. No more distractions banging in my head. I could relax and say my lines.

We got through the shoot. Nic Cage is still married to his actual wife, though I have to say, I did get a little tingle when I watched his eyes during the playback.

That's it. Ain't no lesson in this chapter. Just a story about how I couldn't do my job until I shared the unbearable weight of my first big O with Nicolas Cage.

BODY YADDI YADDI

PERFORMING STAND-UP IS THE best drug in the world. Doing a good set is like injecting joy straight in my veins. I get high as a mofo. Which explains why I freaked out during COVID lockdowns. I had to go cold turkey. It felt like the virus took away my happiness like those Harry Potter dementors, leaving me cold inside. When I couldn't go out into the world and get onstage in front of a live audience? That was like taking away my crack. I was having such a hard time keeping my high rolling, I had to stop myself from hustling jokes on street corners. *Hey, kid, come here. You want to hear a joke?*

While the clubs were closed, I would go into my bathroom and do a full-on comedy routine just for myself and my toothbrush. When I got bored with that, I went out and did stand-up in my garden for my plants. I called it plant-based comedy. I was out there in the yard practicing my act for my avocado trees. I'll tell you something, my plants were a shitty audience. They didn't laugh. They didn't clap for me. They didn't yell for me. So, I put them all in a smoothie and drank it up.

I was already a fucking mess when COVID crept up on us because, in the previous year, I had put on a bunch of weight—forty pounds, to be exact. I'd (A) quit smoking in 2018, and then (B) fucked up my knee real bad in 2019. A + B = a much heavier me.

I had heard a monster appetite might be a side effect of quitting cigarettes, and I am here to tell you that shit is true. To stop smoking, I watched a YouTube video that promised to hypnotize me overnight while I slept. I would lay my head on my satin pillowcase while this British dude whispered, *"You feel peaceful. Let yourself completely relax. You feel comfortable. You have the power and motivation to resist cigarette cravings. You are happier without smoking."*

It might sound like bullshit, but it turned out to be very effective to have an off-brand Hugh Grant talking to me while I was unconscious. After five nights, *boom*, I stopped smoking. No more cigarettes. Thing is, I think my guy was also whispering in my ear about pot pies. I didn't want to smoke anymore, but I did want to EAT.

I ate like I was Jabba the Hutt and Cookie Monster's science baby. I ate up chicken soup, lentil soup, Snickers, scrambled eggs, fried red snapper from Mel's Fish Shack, biscuits and gravy, beef jerky, corned beef and cabbage, hamburger patties, dried apricots with almonds, Fruit by the Foot, steak, lobster, and chicken and dumplings—all before dinner, which would be a bunch of pastrami and some pickles. I love pickles of all kinds—pickled okra, pickled green beans, pickled watermelon rind. Those are some flavors to savor. Then for dessert, I'd bite off the top of one of those dill pickles that come in a big jar and put a Now and Later, Jolly Rancher, or peppermint on top of it.

Sounds like diabetes. Tastes like success.

It got to where I was eating so much, I would fall asleep while I was eating. One morning, I woke up with salami on my face. Not a human salami. A garlic salami. Another day, I made fifteen pounds of brisket and ate that whole thing myself. It was good as hell. My bathroom didn't smell so good the next day, but at least I wasn't smoking.

If you look back at my pictures from that time in my life, it looks like I had eight or ten extra pounds in my neck alone. I did Stephen Colbert's show, and the next day, I had people hitting me in my DMs, saying, "Yo, Tiffany, I think you got a thyroid problem." I went to my doctor. Only problem I had with my thyroid was it kept letting all that food pass by.

Then I tore my meniscus. That's a little piece of cartilage in your knee that keeps your bones from rubbing together. I'd been rehearsing *Black Mitzvah,* and I was doing my joke about how when you have sex with a fat guy, you lift up his belly so you can sit on his dick, and then his belly flops back and locks you in place like the safety bar on a roller coaster. You can be riding that D, and you're not going to fall off for nothing 'cause that belly has you wedged in good. But with a skinny guy, you get on, and when he starts bucking, you're about to slide off his scrawny ass like, "Whoa, nelly!" because there's no belly to hold you in place. When I got to that part onstage, I went to act like I was falling off a skinny dude as we were fucking. I lifted one leg way up and my other foot went *woop*, right out from under me. Mind you, I was wearing four-inch heels, so I bit the dust like I was hungry for it.

That knocked the wind right out of my lungs, but I shook it off, got back up. I finished rehearsal, no problem. But the next night when I was doing the actual show we were recording for Netflix, I did that joke and—*bam*—I fell *again.* The most pain I've ever experienced in my life shot up my leg—*zoom, pow!* I guess God don't like when you joke about fat men.

When I came off the stage, my knee was fucking huge. I didn't even have a knee. It swelled up to the size of my calf so my leg went straight down to the floor like how a three-year-old would draw it. I was mad as hell. I used to have good knees when I was younger. I jumped six feet doing track and field at El Camino Real High School—check the records—but after that fall I could barely walk. If I couldn't walk, I couldn't perform. If I couldn't perform, we were going to have a problem. The lowest times in my life have been when I have not been able to perform comedy. I *needed* to be up on that stage.

I did everything I could think of. I went to doctors, did acupuncture, and got physical therapy. I tried something called scraping where they run a dull blade over your skin to break up the scar tissue underneath, and I gave that knee a lot of rest. While I was resting, I kept eating. I gained more weight. Dat ass got bigger. When I walked around with no panties on, that mothafucka gave me a round of applause everywhere I went. *Step, clap, step clap, step, clap clap clap.* I had my own personal cheering section.

For a while, I didn't let it bother me. I know how to wear weight. I don't mind if I've got a little belly that jiggles and makes my whole aura shimmy when I move. I can carry a few extra pounds and people still compliment me. You don't need to be skinny to be healthy or to look good. There was just a little more of me to love. I thought, *I am perfect the way I am. Anyone says different I'ma pop them in the mouth.*

But then I started to hurt.

I was carrying around the equivalent of a six-year-old with me everywhere I went, and my joints started complaining. "Ho, you not going to be able to live this life."

The strain was not only hurting my body, it was inflicting pain on my spirit. COVID had been hard enough as it was with the world turned upside down, but with my instrument out of whack, my energy was sagging and my soul was dragging, which made it difficult for me to perform even for my plants. I wasn't doing much of anything. I was a slug on a rug.

After a few months without performing, I got to feeling very low down. My blankets felt like they weighed a thousand pounds. I did not want to get up.

Your body is a strong vessel, but that doesn't mean it can't break. You have to take care of it. Just like you have to change the oil in your car. I see guys wipe their car down like, "Look at you, Bessy, you're beautiful." That is an inanimate object. It's just a car. It doesn't have any feelings. We should be loving on our bodies that same way, appreciating how they get us where we need to go.

Finally, I had a *That's So Raven* moment where I went inside my head to talk to myself: "What are you doing, girl? Why are you still lying in this bed? Listen, you are amazing at making people feel good with your comedy. But if you are not able to get out of bed in the morning, you can't share joy with the world. You can't even share your farts. You need to remind this body that you care."

My brain pep talk worked.

I decided to start eating healthier and cut out the foods that were weighing me down so my meat suit could operate at its highest level. I made up my mind to go thirty days completely vegan. I made juice out of everything you can think of—celery, beets, avocado, carrots, peaches, apples. If it came out of the dirt, I put it in the blender.

But something inside me was not happy. My gut parasites wanted steak all the damn time. If my stomach didn't get that meat, it would go *Budauuerghnbenerrrgg. I'm going to mess you up, bitch.* But if I was going to get back onstage, I knew I had to have a talk with my stomach.

TIFFANY: Listen up. Today, we eating out the garden.

STOMACH: Oh, you a comedian, huh? Very funny. Now go cook me up some pastrami.

TIFFANY: Do I look like a short order cook? I'm in charge of this body, starting with what goes in the mouth, and what goes in the mouth today is vegetables. Maybe some fruit. That's it. Or . . . you can go hungry.

STOMACH: [Growls] Fine. But can you at least put some bugs on it?

While I was eating better, I got on the body transformation tip to get myself shredded. I ain't a fan of the gym. I don't like when people look at me while I'm working out. When I lift weights, I make weird noises. I grunt—*errrrrrghhh, ugh, ugh, ahhhhh.* The men in the weight section look at me like, "Is this bitch about to have a baby? Do we need to get some hot water? Call the damn midwife already."

I started waking up early to get in my workout before I began my day. I started running. I did the treadmill for a few weeks. When it was time to put on my sports bra, I'd hear a voice saying, "That's all right, Tiffany. You don't have to get on that treadmill today." That was like a spam call from the devil, so I blocked it. Eventually, I headed down to the beach. (Running on sand will *wipe you out.*) I did planks, butt kicks, squats. You name it. What really killed me were the donkey kicks where you get down on the floor and put all your weight in your arms as you kick your legs up in the air. *Hee-haw!* Every time I went to do those donkey kicks, my joints and muscles said, "What the hell? I thought we had a deal. You were going to get healthy so we have to do *less* work, not more." My legs protested. "*Nooo,* we don't wanna." But I'm in control of my mind, and my mind controls my body, so I said, "No, legs, you going to work today. Get to it." The booty, the abdominals, the thighs, they were all screaming at me. My whole body ached.

It was not fun, y'all. There was definitely crying.

I told myself, "Listen, Tiffany, change is uncomfortable. If you got to do it kicking and screaming, kick and scream. But get with it."

After a couple months, my jeans got loose. My knees felt better. I looked in the mirror and went, *I'm gonna be walking round with my stomach out, looking like Aaliyah. I'm going to be one in a million. These thighs are strong like a thoroughbred.*

There was still a thin layer of fat on me 'cause I'm not out here trying to be a skeleton, but I really got this body tuned up. My instrument felt stronger, and my energy returned.

When some of the COVID restrictions relaxed in 2021, the Laugh Factory opened up. They called me and asked if I wanted to do a set. Fuck yeah, I wanted to do a set. Now that I had my body together, I was ready to light some motherfuckers up. I needed to feel good to be onstage, and I needed to be onstage to feel good. Let's do this.

The night of the show, there was energy coursing through my veins again.

I waited in the wings for the MC to introduce me, bouncing from foot to foot like Muhammad Ali. When it was my time, I came out swinging.

I took off my jacket like I owned the place and shouted, "What's up, Laugh Factory?"

I ain't gonna lie to you all—that was the loudest I've heard a crowd, ever. It felt so good. I was trying not to cry. The audience started standing up. Every last one of them, like they were under mind control.

Before I made a single joke, I knew I had it. I had a room full of strangers in alignment, hanging off every word. Every move I made with that body was the right one, like where time slows down in *The Matrix* so Keanu can dodge bullets or throw the right punch. I'd treated my body right, and now I was able to use it to do what God had put me here to do. There's nothing better than that feeling. It's better than winning a Grammy. Better than a cigarette. Better than sex with a fat man.

I SEE YOU, SOUTH CENTRAL

WHEN I TELL PEOPLE where I live, something happens to their face like I just let one out and they don't know whether to acknowledge the ramen smell that just came out of my ass. They hear "South Central," and they think *gangsters, gunfire, poverty, homelessness—danger*! They think *Boyz n the Hood*. Cars with hydraulics. *Menace II Society* and NWA. Metal fences around front yards. Dudes with 40s of malt liquor in their hands, basketball hoops with no nets, ladies with their hair in curlers and menthol cigarettes dangling as they yell they'll whup their kids' asses if they don't get in the house *right this minute*. Those people with the scrunched-up noses? Most of them have probably never even set foot in South Central. They're just basing their reactions on a bunch of stereotypes. Even those who have been through my neighborhood let those stereotypes cloud their vision, so they don't see what I see. I love it here—the history, the energy, the community. It is my home, and there is nowhere else I would rather be.

After the 2020 Golden Globes ceremony, I could have gone any-where—a banging club, some celebrity after-party—but I came back to the hood to hang with my friends and eat tacos. Because I know where I belong.

When I bought my first house back in 2015, it was my dream house, just a hop, skip, and a jump from where I'd grown up in my grandma's place over on Fifty-Fourth. It was a simple house. No in-ground swimming pool or screening room or any of that *Cribs* shit, but I had 2,200 square feet, a backyard, multiple bedrooms, and even an itty-bitty porch. I worked a long time to be able to own property instead of scraping together rent payments to hand over to a landlord every month. Now I'm enjoying being queen of my castle. Lying in my grass in the backyard on a clear blue day makes me extremely happy.

They call where I live South Central Los Angeles, but it's not really that south in terms of the layout of the city if you get technical with it. I think they called it that because a lot of Black people who were from the South moved into the area when they came out to California. My grandma's people were part of that wave. They came to California in wagons from Kentucky. Or maybe just because it's south of the 10 freeway, the line white residents won't cross because they think that's where the city turns into "the hood." Really, South Central is right in the middle of the city, more central than south. Actually, people use the term "South Central" to refer to pretty much any Black neighborhood in the vicinity—from Watts and Compton to Inglewood and Crenshaw.

You probably don't know this, but South Central is the safest part of Los Angeles—maybe not in terms of the crime rate and people busting into houses and people doing drugs in broad daylight, but in the environmental way. California is cracked with fault lines that could break open and swallow you up at any time, including in LA, but the fault lines don't cut up South Central. The lines run around the neighborhood, not through it. In '94, when the big earthquake hit, whole buildings in the city collapsed like soufflés. A cop car fell off an overpass. Roads crumpled. Fifty-four people died that day. I slept right through it—didn't feel a thing—because my neighborhood was in a safe pocket, a part of the city God smiles on. He shows us He thinks we're special in all kinds of ways. When the fog rolls into Los Angeles, it doesn't really spill into the South Central area. The neighborhood has got the right level of elevation, so if the city floods, we're still going to be sitting there nice and dry. 'Cause it's blessed.

The love I have for my neighborhood can be hard for people to understand. After we did *Girls Trip* together, one of my celebrity friends told me, "Tiffany, you're going to have to move now that you're famous. There's going to be men sitting outside your house with their dicks in their hand. You can't live over there off Crenshaw anymore. You need to move closer to me. Girl, there's mansions over here!"

Buy a house where they have those celebrity home tours and the buses drive by your gate so tourists can try to get a look at you in your bathrobe? I don't think so. I don't want people snooping on me. Part of what I love about where I live is the freedom. I feel safer in my community than I do in The Hills. I match here. I could go out in my garden buck naked and dance the Nae Nae if I want to, and ain't nobody gonna bother me. I go across Wilshire and, all of a sudden, I stick out. Anytime I go where it's a lot of white people, it feels like I draw unwanted attention.

I remember I used to go visit my friend and her kids in El Segundo, which is in Santa Monica. I'd spend the afternoon with her family in their backyard. On my way home, I'd only go a few blocks before there'd be lights flashing in my rearview. I got pulled over by the cops so many times for being in that community, I learned the officers' names. I even dated one of them for a minute. That doesn't happen when I'm hanging out in Crenshaw.

My neighborhood is also mad convenient. Everything is within walking distance. I can leave my house on foot and get to the grocery store in minutes. I can wash my ass, walk out my door, and be at a beauty supply store or a 7-Eleven before my coochie is dry. If my washer and dryer break, I can walk to the laundromat. When you go up in Beverly Hills, you can't walk to shit. I mean you could, but it's going to take a long time. You would have legs of a mountain climber if you walked everywhere up there.

The hills of Beverly are not for me. I don't want to live somewhere where the attic bathroom has a bidet. They don't even have roaches over that way; they have shiny metal-looking beetles. They have raccoons and deer and shit. All kinds of wildlife. I don't like that. I like my wildlife to be crackheads.

There was a lot of wildlife right outside my door as I was growing up. It was the goddamn wild, wild west. I got to meet drug dealers, hustlers, and pimps galore. I was here for the gang wars. That red and blue thing was for real. What you wore could be a full problem. You might have gotten banged on if some crazy-ass gangster came in from the other side of Wilshire and didn't like what you had on. We wore a lot of gray.

With its wide boulevards and palm trees, South Central looks very beautiful. The houses are painted all these different colors—peach and lavender and bright blue—and people have nice grass lawns. In fact, if you squint, it could be the suburbs—but to the gangbangers, it wasn't real estate. It was territory. And that territory needed to be claimed and defended. They were fighting in the streets. Fighting over dope money. Fighting over bitches. And fighting over who controlled the crack.

The crack epidemic hit home for me because, back in the day, my auntie was on crack. She got shot in the back by her dealer. The really sad thing was that she had recently stopped doing crack, but her dealer wanted her to be his girl. She told him, "I'm not about that life no more. We can be cool, but I'm not fucking with you like that." She walked out of the house, and he shot her in the back. *Pop.* She died four hours later.

I definitely saw some shit.

But at the same time, when I lived on Fifty-Fourth, there were a lot of kids—mostly Black, some Hispanic—running around on the block who all played with each other every day. We'd be out there in the mud, letting it dry on our skin, so we cracked like a dried-up creek. We'd play pretend grocery store, running our businesses, and house, creating our families.

My mom used to drop my two sisters, my two brothers, and me off at the McDonald's playground and come back two or three hours later and get us. She gave us five dollars each so we could get whatever we wanted, which made me feel rich as hell. Sometimes we would share our french fries with other kids.

We'd go down to the swap meets to bargain for whatever we needed. If you have never been to a swap meet, it's like a flea market with booths and tables set up for vendors. Part of the game is to try to talk somebody down. You'd be like, "Let me get twenty pair of socks for seven dollars."

"No, no, you pay ten dollars."

"Throw in a pair of those shorts, and I'll pay ten."

"Deal."

On nice days, which was a lot of the time in Los Angeles, I used to ride my tricycle between my mama's house and my grandma's house, pretending like I was about to be on *Star Search*. "Ladies and gentlemen, Tiffany Haddish will be performing soon. Everyone, please come out. Please come to the show." Then I'd go in my back-yard and ride in a circle singing "The Muffin Man" at the top of my lungs. When we got older, some of the kids played Hide and Go Get Her, but they wouldn't let me play because my mama had a reputation for being so mean. They'd say, "You stay at the base, Tiffany." I was just happy to be included.

Us kids would hit up the candy house multiple times a day. The candy house was the house in a neighborhood where you could go knock on the side window and a woman, usually either an older lady or a woman with a gang of kids, would come out. "What the hell you want?" Then she'd sell you a Kool-Aid popsicle from a Dixie cup for a quarter or three Now and Laters for ten cents. You could get a bag of Doritos with chili on top or a bunch of Blow Pops.

That actually inspired one of my first businesses. My friend and I took the candy sales to the streets. We'd buy a box of Blow Pops and another box of Jolly Rancher sticks. We'd go to her house 'cause mine had too many roaches in it, and we'd put the Jolly Ranchers in a bag and drop that bag in boiling water until the candy softened. Then we'd take them out and wrap them around the middle of a Blow Pop. We put 'em in a baggie with a twisty on it and called them Saturn Pops. We sold them for a dollar each. That's how we got the money for our Arizona jean jackets and backpacks.

I'm telling you, my neighborhood was a real-life *Sesame Street*— only the grown-up Cookie Monsters had special cookies with weed in them.

When I was about seven years old, my stepdad got one of my mom's employees pregnant, so they left that mess behind and moved our family out of our community to Pomona, which was a mostly white neighborhood. The day we pulled up in front of our new house, I got out of my car and swore I was at the Nickelodeon awards. I had never seen so many white people outside of the television. Until we moved, I thought teachers all worked on PBS. I'd thought all the police were from *Chips*. When they'd come to my house looking for my auntie, 'cause she was mixed up in some dope shit, I'd go, "Yo, can I get your autograph?"

We moved back to the old block in the early '90s, a few years after my mom's accident. This time around, me and my brothers and sisters weren't allowed outside anymore. The crack years had come on hard, unemployment was really high, and a lot of people were struggling and angry. Too many people had been getting shot, and my family was not having any of that. We had to play inside so we didn't get caught up in the bullshit on the streets, so we were all at home when they read the Rodney King verdict. You can't bring up South Central without talking about the riots. That went down when I was in seventh grade, April 29, 1992.

After that verdict came out, protests exploded instantly. People poured into the streets to release the pressure they felt inside, setting fires, breaking into stores, taking stuff away from other people the way their humanity had been taken from them. Most people around the country heard about what was happening on the news, watching from their couches as fires burned and armed store owners crawled up on roofs. But in my neighborhood, we *heard* it, we *smelled* it. The burning drifted through the streets while the power was out. Low, heavy smoke crawled in through the windows, stinging our noses. People were outside yelling as they ran out their anger at how fucked up the world was that a Black man could get beat like that by three white police and one Hispanic cop, have it recorded, have it played five hundred million times for the whole world to see, only to learn that a mostly white jury found the men who did it innocent. Helplessness burned in people's veins. The National Guard walked the streets of Los Angeles with their weapons out like they were at war. Sixty people lost their lives.

I was only twelve years old. I wasn't trying to protest anything. I wasn't trying to set anything on fire. I just wanted to get some free stuff. For the next two days, I watched through our windows as kids from the neighborhood walked by with Payless shoeboxes and all kind of clothes from Big Lots and Pick 'n Save. People had big turkeys they had boosted from the grocery store, piles of toilet paper, even TVs under their arms. I looked at the parade of people marching by, staggering under the weight of all the stuff they'd grabbed, and said to my mama, "They looting! Let's go to that Payless. I need shoes."

My mama did not let one goddamn second pass before she said, "No, we don't participate in that kind of foolishness." That was the end of it for her.

Schools closed for a week, and the city implemented a curfew while shit was going down. After things had cooled off a bit, my family piled in the car, a green hatchback with plastic seats that had flowers on them. That car was so ugly, it was called the Gremlin. We drove around the neighborhood in the Gremlin and saw how much had been burned down. The swap meet on Vermont burned down. The Crenshaw Mall. The Shell station. The ground was black and charred like a volcano, and glass was everywhere.

When we went back to school, everybody's hair looked so good because they had stolen perm kits. Kids were dressed in cute outfits their mamas stole for them. They had new backpacks, new shoes, new everything. I didn't have shit.

I came home at the end of my first day back at school angry as hell. "Mama, this is how I know you don't love me, 'cause you didn't go out and steal for us. I still have shoes with holes in them." If it hadn't been for my mama, I would have been one of those looters—not because of my righteous anger but because I thought I needed some new Looney Tunes sneakers.

That video, that verdict, those riots, they really set the tone for a fucked-up relationship between police and residents of South Central.

Generally speaking, I try not to call the cops because they just bring more trouble. Though the other day, I did dial the cops because I saw the craziest shit. I had come home after a late night. At one o'clock in the morning, I looked out the window. There went a white lady pushing her expensive baby stroller and walking her dog down my street in the black of night. My first thought when I saw that white lady was, *Either she's selling drugs or she's not right.* I called 911. They showed up quick. The last two years they've been coming way faster than they have in the past—and I'm not even dating any of 'em.

But it turns out she was just taking her baby for a stroll. The fact that a white lady felt safe doing that down my block at 1:00 a.m.? That made me feel some kind of way.

I'm definitely starting to see more white people over here where I live. A couple years ago, census workers came to my house because they wanted to see how many Black people were in my neighborhood. The dude asked me what race I was. "What race? Is you colorblind?" Ten years ago, they wouldn't have needed to send anyone out for the count. The census workers could have just stayed home and checked off Black, Black, Black, Black, and Black, all the way down. But not anymore. It started out as just a sprinkling—two or three white faces in the crowd—but it's like someone dumped the whole jar of sprinkles all over these streets and now they're glistening like the beach. Feels like every new person who moves into my hood is white. I joke that when I dyed my hair blond, I did it to fit in with my new community. The property values have gone up, but the neighborhood has changed. You don't see as many gangbangers. Now it's the real estate agents who are claiming their turf. The area is transforming. They're selling these houses around me. The agents are saying, "Tiffany Haddish lives in this neighborhood!" like I'm a selling point. Every time someone moves in, there is a pie or cake at my front door. There are only three Black families on the block now. Everybody else is white, Hispanic, or Asian.

Even the Jungle right down the street from my house where *Training Day* was set, that's changed. You can drive around at 2:00 a.m. without worrying about anybody shooting at your car. Used to be, if you found yourself in trouble over there, police showed up and they'd be like, "Well, you should have known better."

There's no rent control around here, so these luxury condos are spreading like a fungus across the neighborhood. There is a Starbucks down the street. They're redoing the Crenshaw Mall and building a five-star hotel. Inglewood is now home to SoFi Stadium, which cost multiple billions of dollars to build. They're about to put a Kaiser Permanente in the neighborhood. That's how you really know the white people are moving in.

New things can't move in without old things moving out. There's not as many swap meets as there used to be. The Payless shoe store is gone, Fedco, Big Lots. Yeah, those aren't little mom-and-pop shops, but they served the community more than some store that sells twelve-dollar beers ever could. You know what else is gone? The candy houses.

That's how gentrification works, right? Someone sniffs around, smells some cheap real estate, and scoops it up. They raise the rent so the only people who can afford it are people with that generational wealth, which is hard to get when your ancestors weren't allowed to own land until around a hundred years ago. There are housing deeds in this city that still say, "No lot in said tract shall at any time be lived upon by a person whose blood is not entirely that of the Caucasian race."*

Those words don't hold up in court anymore, but that sentiment has hung around like a fart in church.

There have been a lot of open houses in the area recently, but the people I've seen getting out of their Priuses and Teslas for tours have not been people whose families have lived here for decades. They've been white dudes with soccer player haircuts. When property turns over, the neighborhood starts to cater to that new crowd. Now you've got a situation where the old-timers not only can't afford what these new stores are selling, but they don't feel welcome in them either—*in their own neighborhood.* There are stores where they have code names for Black people who they think are going to shoplift for no reason

* Ryan Reft, "How Prop 14 Shaped California's Racial Covenants," KCET, September 20, 2017, https://www.kcet.org/shows/city-rising/how-prop-14-shaped-californias-racial-covenants.

other than they walked through the door. That shit will make you feel unwanted. So, when grandma dies and it was her name on the lease, the rest of the family who were living with her go, "We got two choices: We could keep renting here among the boba tea shops and infrared light studios, whatever the fuck that is, or we could move with all the other Black people over to Lancaster or San Bernardino and save a bunch of money." After they move out, the owners take the Section 8 off the property, do some renovations, and rent it to more rich folks. Before you know it, you got a whole new population. There are just not as many people who look like me in my neighborhood as there used to be. There are days where I'm like, "Where did everybody go? Did everybody die?"

I never thought it would happen here. But I've been in this neighborhood my whole life and I'm not going anywhere.

When I was younger, I watched celebrities who came up in my neighborhood. Soon as they had it made, they went, "It's been real, but I'm out." I always wondered why they moved out of the hood like they wanted to forget about us as quick as possible. Why be successful and run away from who you are and where you're from? Why not stay and reinvest in the place that made you? That's why I haven't moved out. I want to be an example to my community. That way, the kids who are growing up here can see me and go, "If Tiffany Haddish can do it, anybody can. If she stuck around, we must be worth staying for."

What those people who keep trying to get me to move to the Hills don't see is the stuff I love best about my neighborhood: the part of the hood that's still hanging on by its teeth, keeping it real.

Like the other day, there was a little block party one block over from where I live. Not an official block party where they shut down the street with a permit and put up the barricades but probably four or five families who set tables out front of their house, put up little tents—the gazebo things—like a pop-up party.

Kids were playing, chasing each other up and down the street. One of the neighbors, he had his speakers out and he was DJing, playing Bobby Brown, Ginuwine, Usher, all the songs from the '90s and early 2000s. It felt like I was back in high school. The vibe was just family, dancing, and having fun.

They got the Juicy Burger truck on the corner. Coolers dotting the sidewalk. Some people pulled chairs out into the street while others sat on their porches talking to each other and going from house to house visiting like they were on an episode of *227*, checking in with each other, being neighborly. It was such a nice scene. There's no way I'm going to find that kind of joy anywhere else.

You wouldn't see that in those big old mansions in Beverly Hills. Can you imagine? "Okay, we're going to have a party in the front yard, but please don't trample my heritage grass. Can you ask Anders to move the tent so it doesn't block the Cayenne?"

Here, people were singing along, dancing in their shorts, not caring if their booty was hanging out as they laughed with their neighbors. That was beautiful. That's my neighborhood. I will stay here until I'm old as hell, rolling my wheelchair down Crenshaw, playing some old songs, selling Saturn Pops, and asking everyone if they want to come hear me sing the shit out of "The Muffin Man."

TEA WITH AN OG

IT WAS A GOOD day for boo-tay. The air was crisp and snappy, and I had that pre-shoot energy humming. It was the fall of 2019, and I was in New York City to shoot a movie. If you know me at all, you know I am LA all day, but I like New York because it's easy to pick up men there, especially when it's cold out because they're looking for someone to snuggle up with. I didn't have time on this trip to get dressed to go out to the clubs to sample what New York had to offer because we would be doing long days of production for the movie. But I did have time for some dibble-dabbling on Bumble. I'd downloaded the app the night before on my first day in town, swiping by this guy and that guy. No one caught my eye, until . . . hold up. I stopped on a profile of this dude who had big white teeth and hair like Ben Affleck. I recognized this dude—let's just call him Ben. He'd been in the audience of one of my comedy shows the last time I was in New York.

How about that? You never know who is going to turn up on the apps. We'd talked a little after my set 'cause I'd thought he was cute, plus he was in real estate and I believe in buying land, so I'd given him my number. I was headed back to LA the next morning so we hadn't gotten together, but now here I was back in New York, so what the hell? I went ahead and liked him on the app. Within an hour, he called me, and we made plans for him to come back to chill in my room after I was done shooting the next day—by which I meant I planned to turn on *Game of Thrones* while I let him eat me out. Thank you, New York.

On that second day in New York, I walked into my hotel after wrapping for the day when the doorman stopped me.

"Excuse me, Ms. Haddish, someone wants to talk to you." He actually said the name of an A-list celebrity. I'm going to call her OG Hollywood Celebrity.

The fuck? I didn't know this woman. I mean, I knew who she *was*, but we weren't girls or anything. I was aware she was one of the other actors in the movie I was shooting, but we didn't have real scenes together. I knew from the script there'd be times when our characters would be in the same room, but we weren't in the same situation. (That's a little foreshadowing right there, y'all.)

The doorman gave me her room number and said, "Call her."

I took the number, but it was after ten o'clock at night and I had Ben coming over, so I said to myself, *I'm not calling OG Hollywood Celebrity this late. I'll hit her up another time.*

I went up to my room to unwind. My room was niiiiiice, like out of a magazine. There were little decorative objects on the tables and shit. I even had an extra bedroom and a kitchen to myself. Ben came over, and let's just say I didn't give another thought to OG Hollywood Celebrity that night.

The next day, I went to work, shot my scenes, and came back to my hotel. But when I got there, the same doorman stopped me again. "OG Hollywood Celebrity really wants you to call her. Here's her cell phone number."

Seriously? What was she about? I knew she had a cousin who was a comedian, so maybe she wanted to talk to me about that? I took the number and debated whether to call her. I considered it. After all, she *had* given her cell number to the doorman, but I didn't need anybody on set talking about how I woke up this famous white lady in the middle of the night. I had too much sense for that, so I just went to sleep.

Okay, so then the *next* day after work, when I got back to my room, there was a voice mail message, saying, "Girl, it's OG Hollywood Celebrity. Call me."

Damn. I guess she really did want to talk.

I dialed her number, but she didn't answer. So maybe she didn't want to talk that bad? That was all right by me because Ben was on his way over again. I washed my ass while I waited for him to get his ass up to my room. A few minutes later, I let him in, and we started getting into it real quick. We were headed to the couch when the phone rang. When I answered, there was OG Hollywood Celebrity on the other end.

"Honey, I'm sorry I missed your call. I want us to get together. Where are we drinking marijuana tea? My room or yours?"

Mind you, I never met this woman before, and I was about ten minutes away from fucking, but how am I going to say no to an offer like that?

"What floor are you on?"

"I'm in the penthouse."

"The penthouse? I'm only on the eighth floor. We doing it in your room."

I hung up and looked over at Ben, who had taken the liberty of getting butt-ass naked while I was on the phone. He was looking at me like he was ready to get busy, but I said, "I'm sorry. I gotta go talk to OG Hollywood Celebrity right now. I'll be right back."

"Can I come with you?"

"What? Hell no. I'm not bringing one of the Property Brothers up to meet OG Hollywood Celebrity. You wait here."

I was already mostly undressed myself, so I put on the cushy hotel bathrobe and started to head up to her room. But then I thought, *I don't know if I should go meet OG Hollywood Celebrity, who is pretty much a legend, in a damn robe.* I stood there thinking about what to put on to go meet with a famous actress at eleven o'clock at night.

As I was hemming and hawing, she called again and asked, "How long is it going to take you to get up here? Jeez, what are you doing?"

"Girl, I'm trying to decide what to put on. All I got on is a robe, and I don't want to come in your room in a robe."

"I don't care what you've got on, just come up here." So, I threw on a T-shirt and some pants and then I put the robe on over it.

We all got our reputations, you know? Like I'm known for being fun, funny, and a little crazy. Not like slash-your-tires crazy. More like dance-at-the-church-service crazy or jump-out-the-car-at-a-stoplight-and-start-popping-my-booty-like-*She-ready!* crazy. OG Hollywood Celebrity has played a lot of strong women, and in the movie we were doing, she was basically playing herself—a real self-possessed well-known actress. So, on my way up to her room, I imagined I would find her sitting there in a tailored shirt ready to greet me with a Katharine Hepburn voice. "Tiffany, darling, how are you, my dear? You must tell me about your life. Who are you *really?*"

But when she opened the door, there she was in her comfy clothes, real chill, like, "Hey, girl, how are you?" She invited me in and started talking to me like we'd known each other forever—telling me how her day was, how shooting went for her, about this event she had gone to, this and that. I was listening, but I'm going to be honest with you. I wasn't hearing everything. I was too busy looking around her room. The penthouse was fly as hell. Her room didn't just have nice art objects, it had *stairs*. It was like a full duplex apartment. I made a note to myself. *Man, I got to get my status up so I can get me a room like this.* OG Hollywood Celebrity noticed me looking around and said, "You want a tour? Go on. Check it out."

So, we went upstairs and into her bedroom. (Don't get excited. This isn't that kind of story.) I was touring the real estate—maybe I should have brought Ben with me after all. I stood at the foot of her bed and looked out. You could see the whole city—the Empire State Building over here, the Chrysler Building over there. All these glistening lights. It was really, really nice. On my way out, I looked in the bathroom. There were blond hair pieces spread out all over the counters. She was kind of apologetic. "I took my hair out."

"Girl, I understand. You come in my bathroom, and you'll see so many wigs and hair pieces you'd be afraid. You'd be like, 'What the fuck is that? A mongoose?'"

She laughed, and we started back down the stairs. I was ready to say, "Okay, thanks for the tour. I'll see you tomorrow," but she said, "Now, let's have our tea."

"Oh yes, our tea!"

We sat down, and she poured tea in a mug for me. I offered her the little two-hitter roach joint I'd brought with me.

We smoked and drank tea. I was feeling very relaxed when she started saying how me and her had so much in common. I looked at her like, *Really, Miss Penthouse? You been in foster care? You ever wake up with police in your face because you slept in your car?*

I said, "For real? What you and I got in common?"

"I've been working on writing my book, and I read yours. It really inspired me as I was telling my story."

I was very open and honest about my life in *The Last Black Unicorn.* I tried to keep it funny, but I put it all out there. I got real about how my mama's accident fucked her up and how that fucked me up. I didn't see what OG Hollywood Celebrity had found in my book that reminded her of her own life, but then she said, "My mom also had some mental issues. I didn't understand what she was going through at the time. Not until I got older."

What do you know? We did have something in common after all. She told me so many things I never knew about her that were really similar to things I'd gone through. I looked at her like, *Wow. Me and this white lady* do *have a lot in common. We are two peas in a pod.*

The more she talked, the more I was there for it. I was digging it, listening to every single word. I sank into her sofa as the tea kicked in, and I got real sleepy, almost drifting off, bobbing my head. Might have been the tea. Might have been the fact that it was late as hell. I curled up into my robe and thought, *Man, it don't matter what color your skin is. It don't matter where you grow up or what kind of money you have. There is probably something you have in common with everybody. There's a common ground under our feet somewhere.*

I use that connection to other people in my acting career. Every time I play a new character, I do a lot of work to prepare for the role. The way I see it is that every script is a slice of someone's life, and if I'm going to do a good job, I've got to know about that life. Where did they come from? Where did they go? I have a notebook about my character's thoughts, how she feels, what she thinks about. I try to guess how she would dress. If she was going to a party, would she wear a dress or a jumpsuit? Or does she hate parties? I'll imagine what her take on some political thing is, what she likes to eat, what pisses her off. I write in my diary from the perspective of that character. I zoom in and I try to figure out how aspects of this character relate to me.

It's totally a human experience to try to get inside somebody else's head and figure out what you share. I was enjoying sitting across from OG Hollywood Celebrity, finding the me in her, connecting. I thought, *We are all linked up in here.*

Then she hit me with "You know, Jane Fonda and I, we've been talking. Jane has been doing this thing about climate change where she protests in front of the White House and gets arrested every Friday. It's called Fire Drill Fridays."

That woke me right up.

"Bitch, you shouldn't get arrested for protesting," I said.

"Well, we *are* protesting in front of the White House. They do arrest people for that."

Maybe that tea was stronger than I thought. I had to clarify. "You're getting arrested *intentionally*? Like, by your own choice?"

"Yeah . . . You should come a couple of Fridays and do it with us."

I got real quiet. I looked side to side like, *Okay, where are the cameras? I know Ashton Kutcher about to jump out at me 'cause I'm being Punk'd.* Did she honestly just ask me to go to a protest and get arrested *on purpose?*

I have gone to some protests. With everything that's happened to the Black community over the last few years, I have gotten out there on the streets to show I think the world is messed up as hell and we need some big fucking changes ASAP.

After George Floyd was killed, I went to a protest at the Laugh Factory. The thing about that protest? All the streets were shut down and people knew it was happening. Black Women Lead got those permits. No one was getting arrested. No one was getting their ass beat just for speaking their truth. The organizers at the Laugh Factory invited me to say something, so I stepped up and took the mic for a minute. It felt so good to have a safe space to get my words out. I talked about fear, about hope. I had some other words I would have liked to share with the police, including the ones who were there to keep the peace. I would have loved to fire off cuss words at 'em, *ratatatat.* But I knew better. Ain't no way I could cuss out a cop. You do that as a Black person and *boom*, you're another statistic. That's some white privilege.

Let's get this straight. I don't go anywhere with the intention of *I'm going to get my ass arrested*. There's a chance, sure, but I ain't signing up for it.

So, I told OG Hollywood Celebrity, "Girl, I know I'm Jewish, but you do realize I'm Black, right? You are a white woman. If you go to jail, you're going to get out. Jane Fonda is a white woman. She's going to get out. But if they lock me up? They're going to keep my Black ass all week. Lord knows what kind of incidences I've been associated with. I ain't innocent. They finally get my DNA, they finally get my fingerprints, match them up with some bullshit, they'll be like, 'It's a wrap!' They'll charge me with who knows what! No. I don't feel comfortable with that."

She sat back in her chair, listening. But was she hearing me?

If you're white and you're reading this, I hope you're hearing me.

In 2020, I was invited to attend George Floyd's memorial. I went in support of the family because I know how difficult it is to lose a loved one like that. When I saw police outside the event, it was like the murderer coming back to the scene of the crime. I felt some sort of way about it.

I'm not a fearful person, but my experiences with police have not been good. I have watched my friends be slaughtered by the police. As a thirteen-, fourteen-year-old girl, I had a friend—he wasn't even doing anything, but I guess he looked like somebody. He was just walking, and the police stopped him. They got into a scuffle. There was nothing I could do except yell out, "No, don't do that!" But what was my yelling going to do? And then he was dead. Gone. I saw that happen. My friend had just been walking. Walking while Black. And his story ended right there.

Three years later, another friend was killed by the police for no fucking reason at all. We were on the east side, in Watts. I was hanging out with my cousins, and the police started talking at us. We were calm, cool, and collected. All of a sudden, the police officers just started getting hella aggressive. We were like, "What the hell?" We were kids. All we could do was scream. The police grabbed my friend. They were tussling and then, by the end, he was dead, too. The police officer was on his neck, and he died. He was eighteen or nineteen years old.

At the memorial, all my PTSD came rushing back. It reminded me of all my friends whose funerals I had already went to. Friends I went to school with who died or been locked up for no reason 'cause they couldn't afford a good lawyer or who had been accused of things they didn't do. I cried so much. I was trying to swallow my tears, trying to make my tears go back. They were going back, but they were coming out my nose, and my COVID mask filled up with snot. The next day my face was very soft from my snot facial.

My tears were not just for George Floyd; they were for all the people who've died. When they had those eight minutes and forty-six seconds of silence onstage, I was standing next to the mother of a victim. Through the quiet, I thought about what if someone's knee was on my neck for that long? I thought about how helpless my friends were when they were being attacked. The amount of pain I felt was tremendous. Thing is, you can cry all you want, but it doesn't wash away the world. It was a beautiful service, and I was so grateful that I got to be there.

Shit like that can make you feel like the police have a license to kill us. It's fucking terrifying. White friends have told me when they see police behind them on the highway when they've been speeding, they get a drop feeling in their guts, like they're on a roller-coaster dip. They're afraid they're going to get a ticket. Now, I do not want a speeding ticket either, but Black people get that feeling when we see police when we are not doing a damn thing wrong. You'll be buying an ice cream cone and see a uniform out of the corner of your eye, and your stomach clenches up. You go full fight, flight, or freeze. Heart rate up, little sweat on the lip, woozy feeling in your head. You give a smile like, "Hello there, Officer. I'm just trying to get some butter pecan and I'll be on my way. Please don't shoot me."

Interviewers love to ask if I'm gonna drop some babies, and there have been times where I thought I would like to do that, but I don't think that's my path. I always make up these excuses in the interviews: "Oh, I need a million dollars in the bank before I'm gonna have a baby." Or I'll make up a list of requirements a man would have to fulfill before I would agree to have a baby with him: He has to not have any kids of his own yet, be able to pick me up without making any old man sounds, and have a mole on his left foot. But what it actually boils down to—the real reason I'm not going to have babies— is because I would hate to give birth to someone who looks like me, knowing they're going to be hunted or killed. I don't want the stress of worrying every time my Black baby goes out to school or goes to hang out with their friends that they could end up dead. It feels like they're trying to exterminate us. Trying to make us an endangered species. I have four godbabies, and I'm scared to death for them. I know I am not the only Black woman who feels this way. White people don't have to think about that. OG Hollywood Celebrity didn't have to think about that.

When she asked me to come get arrested with her like it was no big deal, I realized we might have had some of the same experiences, but this woman knew nothing about being Black. I'm not picking on this woman in particular. I'm just saying she don't know. There are some things you cannot know unless you lived them.

It's like, I might have a lot of things in common with a doctor, but I know nothing about actually being a doctor. You know what I'm saying? I've been to a doctor. I can relate to a doctor. Some of my best friends might be doctors, and we might have a nice discussion together. But I don't know what it's like to live as a doctor, to have days where my job is life or death or what it's like to have everyone instantly know that I've gone to college when I introduce myself. Feel me? As much life experience as OG Hollywood Celebrity and I share, she doesn't know what it takes to be Black.

I wasn't about to be the one Black face in the crowd at Jane Fonda's protest.

If you're white, let me ask you something. When was the last time you were the only white person in the room? You had to think a minute, didn't you? I cannot tell you how many times I have been the only person with brown skin in a room. I brought a white friend of mine to a family barbeque a couple months ago. She's usually the life of the party, but I noticed she was sitting in the corner, kind of hunched over. I went over and asked what was wrong.

"Tiffany, I feel really uncomfortable. I just feel like I . . . stand out." You think I didn't feel like I stood out at her birthday dinners where nobody who looked like me was there? Or when I went to her nightclubs and every person there was white? Or when I'm at a meeting and there's not one other Black face in the room? White people are used to having other people from their culture around in most situations.

I remember the first time I was the only Black face in a crowd. When we moved to Pomona right when I started second grade, I had to change schools and the one I ended up at was a white elementary school. From day one, I didn't match. It was this sick feeling of *"I'm not good enough to be here."*

It didn't help that I couldn't read, 'cause it made me feel stupid in class. I looked forward to recess because nobody was asking me to read anything. I didn't have any friends to play with except this one little white girl. For the first two days, I played hopscotch by myself. But on my third day at that new school, I decided, *I got on a pretty dress. I'm going to be out here making friends.*

As a kid, I owned the monkey bars. I could climb across, go backward, spin around, throw my legs up, sit on top, roll back, all kinds of stuff. I thought, *Wait 'til these kids see my skills. Then they'll be lining up to be my friend.* When I got over to the monkey bars, every single kid jumped off like rats from a sinking ship. But I didn't get the message. In my head, I went, *That's right, make some room for the best. I'm about to shine.*

I jumped up and went across, then back the other way. I went to the middle and did my little turn in the circle thing that made my hair spin, and when I released, I landed on one knee like a superhero. I turned to all those little white kids who were watching me and said, "Bet y'all can't do that." And then one boy—he had the most beautiful eyes—said, "You damn right we can't do that. We're not monkeys."

What this funky butt say to me?

"You're a monkey girl."

My one white girlfriend fired back, "She is not a monkey; she's Black."

"Black, monkey, same thing."

What the fuck? Did this dude just compare me to an animal? And it wasn't a horse or a unicorn? I didn't know how to respond, so I turned around and walked away, trying to wrap my head around what had gone down. Was it just him, or did all the white kids at that school hate me? From the number of mean comments I heard in the lunch line when I didn't have money to pay for my food, it felt like maybe it was everyone there looking down on me.

I did eventually find friends, but I never forgot how in one second that boy with the pretty eyes had turned my joy into hurt because he didn't like the color of my skin. It made it very difficult for me to trust kids at that school.

Let me give you a bigger example of how it's just different when you're Black. I watched the Capitol riots go down on January 6, 2021. When all those white people went up there, they walked right past the security standing on the steps. They went past the metal detectors, past the barricades, past everything. They stormed that mother like Dawn of the goddamn Dead. They carried their hatred up into one of the best-guarded buildings in America, climbing the walls like a mess of poisonous spiders. They got up in the faces of the police, yelling and cursing right in their grills. Most of those guards barely did anything. If those had been Black people yelling at them, they'd have dropped bombs on their ass before they even got to the steps.

I couldn't explain the feeling I had watching that happen, not exactly. But it was a *really bad* feeling, like I was under attack. I felt personally violated watching those white supremacists publicly hating everyone who looked like me and no one stopping them. I'm not dumb. I know there are racists in this world, but seeing so many come crawling out of the shadows and into the spotlight in an organized way freaked me the fuck out. How do I know if you are one of the ones who hates me or wants to kill me? Watching that army of white dudes march with their hate flags flying into the center of our government—the institution that is meant to serve all of us, *equally*—knocked something loose in me.

The day after the riots, I woke up shaking in a complete sweat—head to toe. I felt like a bad pimple—red, angry, and about to explode. I wanted to go out in the backyard, rip plants out of the ground, and scream. My body stopped shaking eventually, but my mind was on hyper-drive. I couldn't shut it down. I wanted to open up my head and give my brain away, put the knowledge of how we get treated somewhere I didn't have to think about it, like how we bury nuclear waste.

That day at work on a TV show I was in, I was amped-up, really hostile, like I didn't know if I wanted to fight or what. My senses were on high alert. I looked around and the only Black people on the set that day were the Black people I'd brought with me—my makeup artist, my stylist, and so on. I wondered if I should have brought a gun to work. My mind raced. I looked at all the faces in the room, trying to decide, *Are you for me or against me? What's your agenda, white man? Are you going to gather up the eight Black people that work on this show and put us all in one trailer and throw us off the side of a cliff? Are we safe?* Nobody could look me in my fucking eyes. Right before we did the first take of the first scene, I burst into tears. Big crying, not little cute crying. The floodgates were opened, and there was more snot, too.

The person I was doing the scene with came over and rubbed my back, saying, "It's going to be all right. Girl, I know. I know. I know. I know. I know." But, no, she *don't* know. Like OG Hollywood Celebrity, like every other white person, she don't really know.

So, okay, there are a million things about OG Hollywood Celebrity's life I can't relate to. So, I'm not going to presume anything about what those experiences had been like for her. Best I can do is try to relate, try to put myself in her shoes just like I do when I'm researching a character so I can try to respect that experience, even while I know that's just a slice of the life, not the whole pie. There will be parts of it I'll never know.

Back in that fancy-ass room, when OG Hollywood Celebrity said, "Come on, Tiffany. Protest with us," I told her, "I'll tell you what. You want me to send some money for the earth? I'll write you a check. You want me to post about your cause on Instagram? I'll post it. But I cannot voluntarily be like, 'Yeah, police, come put me in the handcuffs.' The only way I will voluntarily get arrested is if somebody beat the dog shit out of me and I want to murder them. I will take myself to the police station and say, 'Lock me up because I'm going to commit murder. Keep me from killing because I don't want nobody to die.' But other than that situation, I am not about to invite the police to lock me up. 'Cause it's gonna turn out different for me than it is for you."

She looked over the top of her teacup at me. I could see the wheels turning. She said, "You know what? I get it." I started to nod a little bit. "But if you change your mind, we'd love to have you out there with us." She didn't get it.

Listen, I like OG Hollywood Celebrity. I could see her spirit, and I think she's a good person. Like I said, I'm not trying to pick on her in particular. But in that conversation, it was like she cared more about the environment than she did about people. I see this in white people all the time, even in the best-intentioned folks. It's like there's a hole in their thinking. They've got love for the polar bears, for the trees, for electric cars, but when it comes to brown and Black people, they've got a blind spot in their hearts. Nobody wants more hurricanes or hungry polar bears, but maybe if we could not enslave people in jails or if we could get rid of sex slavery or create more jobs or help the homeless so they're not shittin' in the street—maybe if we treated each other a little better, maybe the earth would do better, too.

After I'd said my piece, my phone slid out of my robe pocket onto the couch and I saw it was after 1:00 a.m. in the goddamn morning. I had an early call the next day. Tiredness hit me like a monsoon. I had to get out of there.

OG Hollywood Celebrity and I said our goodbyes, and I made my way back to the eighth floor. I guess that tea was still messing with my head 'cause when I opened the door, I could have sworn there was a white man waiting on my couch, dick dangling like a cat toy.

I'm pretty sure things are gonna change for Black people. But things need to fall apart and get put back together again in a way that's fair. In my gut, I feel like we're gonna look around in five or ten years and see that the world is different. I'm praying it's different for the better 'cause people evolve. Or maybe by then the aliens will show up and give all the Black people superpowers. They'll make it so we can fly, and white people will be like, *Dang, we fucked up. We should have been nicer to them!* They will be out on the street waving their 23andMe results like, "Look, I got 2 percent Black in me! Let me fly."

In the meantime, if you're white and you're reading this, go tell all the other white people. Sure, we got a lot in common, but not everything. Get on that hotline I know you all have where you all talk. Tell them that you cannot know what it's like to be Black unless you are Black. Don't ask us to do things just because you would do them. You need to be making those phone calls to the politicians, to the board supervisors, to the mayors, and tell them to dismantle the systemic racism that has been going on for a long time. You're the ones that created the system in the first place.

But OG Hollywood Celebrity, for real, you're my girl. Call me. We'll have tea.

YOU GET WHAT YOU GIVE

WHENEVER SOMEONE SAYS TO me, "Girl, you came outta nowhere with *Girls Trip!*" I tell them to get the fuck outta here with their "nowhere." I've been in the comedy game since I was sixteen years old, back in 1997. That's the late 1900s—a whole other century. I sweated for a lot of years before I became successful and, to be honest, I'm still sweating. My success was no "overnight sensation," no "out of left field phenomenon," no "lucky break." No. It was a loooooong slow road that I pushed myself down inch by inch with a whole lot of hard work—and a good fucking attitude.

Let me give you the short version of Tiffany Haddish's career path. Coming up, I played a million different small parts on-screen, starting with work as a background actor on television. They call you "actors," but it's more like being a mime or a flagpole because you are supposed to be totally silent. You're basically human filler on the set, but I didn't mind. You could put me in a cafeteria scene or in a crowd at a sporting event, and I had no complaints. I did background work on *The OC, One Tree Hill, Hannah Montana*—all the white shows where they needed one Black girl to walk around not talking.

Actually, I did have one complaint. The thing about being a background actor is that you do a lot of waiting around, which gives you a lot of time to observe. You know what I observed? White people. In front of the camera and behind it. There were not many people who looked like me on those sets. I could play Spot One Single Other Black Actor / Crew Member on This Shoot and *lose*. That didn't sit right with me, but I didn't have any power back then to do a damn thing about it. Nobody wanted to hear from me on camera—and they most definitely didn't want my input off camera—but I made a promise to myself that if I ever did get some power, I was going to add a little color to the scene.

I got booked in a Wes Craven movie and a few other nonspeaking roles in films before I finally got to open my mouth and speak on camera on an episode of *That's So Raven*. I played a tour guide in a bio dome wearing a snappy little blazer. Those thirty seconds of talking about carnivorous plants earned me my SAG card. I was legit—even though I still ended up in roles where my credit was "Urban Girl." But I kept it positive. I did whatever I could to get ahead. A studio needed me to run lines with someone? You got it. Do a table read? I was there. Be a stand-in for someone who was sick or on another shoot? Tiffany Haddish, at your service.

Every set I was on, I made friends. Even when you have a speaking part, there is a lot of downtime when you're filming. I used it to get to know the people I was working with. I try to be friendly to people, make them smile, make them laugh—just make them feel good—and that good energy pays off. To this day, I make friends with the cameraman—not just because he's gonna make me look good but because behind that camera he's a person just like anyone else. I'm down with the craft service people, the gaffers, hair and makeup, the person who comes by with papers who says, "I need you to sign this." Everybody. Whenever someone went out of their way to be nice to me, I told them, "If I ever make it, I'm coming back for you. If I ever get a show of my own, I'm going to put you on."

The whole time I was trying to land roles on-screen, I was doing stand-up whenever I could, flexing my funny, honing my craft, and working my ass off. The big comics, they do ten minutes or even twenty or a full hour, and they make it seem like nothing. What you didn't see was the 750 hours they spent working on their material, sweatin' in smaller clubs and at open mics, trying out jokes that nobody liked and then going home, making them better, and trying again. Jerry Seinfeld has said that comedy is a game of tonnage. You've got to do a billion reps so you can make yourself a beast strong enough to go out and kill.

I am all about getting in my reps. When I got serious about making it in stand-up in the early 2000s, I was doing three shows a night—not for the money, for the experience. As an up-and-comer, they give you $100 for ten shows or two drinks and a chicken dinner for one night. The only real benefit that came with doing those shows was I would get comp tickets to pass out to all the extras I was hanging out with on various sets, and I used every one.

I would hop in my Geo Metro to do a set in Azusa, then I'd hustle over to do one in Hollywood, walk off that stage, and head straight to a club on Pico and La Brea. When I finished, it would be like one o'clock in the morning, and I'd still be out there trying to talk my way into a fourth show at some tiny joint with three people in the audience, two of them passed out on a plate of nachos. Anywhere there was a stage and people were willing to listen, I was ready to perform. I did stand-up in barbershops, in hospitals, at baby showers, in muddy backyards, and even in old folks' homes. Old folks' homes have to be the craziest shows. I did this one where a lady in a flower dress pushed her folding chair up next to a white-haired gentleman in the front row. They were probably in their eighties. About ten minutes into my set, another woman rolled up with her walker and got in the first lady's face, yelling, "Get your Jell-O eating ass away from my man!" She started swatting on this couple, hitting their Yoo-hoos out of their hands onto the floor in the middle of my comedy show. Girlfriend did not let up. She was raining her fists of fury on those old lovebirds. But it was like a slow-motion fight. *Hiiiiiiiiiyaaaaaaaaaaaah.* My guy must have had some fire in his diapers because those women were mad about it. That show was another rep.

To be clear, doing stand-up comedy and background work *does not* pay for your life—unless you got a rich daddy. I did not have a rich daddy. What I had was a day hustle at A Place Called Home, a youth center over on the east side. In 2003, I'd been looking for a new gig after I stopped working at the airlines, and my homegirl was working in the accounting department there. She'd recommended me to work with the kids, teaching dance. I'd put in a full day of work getting jiggy with those kids, then drive over to my auditions, my forehead still shiny with sweat.

Every once in a while, I would take the kids from the youth center to watch the TV shows being taped on lots nearby. I wanted to show them the TV programs they loved were getting made right across town, and they could be a part of that. Studio City was less than an hour away, but it might as well have been in Tokyo. Some of the kids at A Place Called Home were in the foster care system. It didn't occur to them to apply for jobs on TV or movie sets. These kids didn't have Uncle Mort at William Morris going, "Charles, would you like an internship at the agency? Let me make a phone call. Okay. Done. You start Monday."

On the bus on the way over to *One on One* or *In the Cut*, I would hype the kids up. "Your energy is part of what's going to make this show good. All right now, who is going to bring that energy? When they have a dance contest, who gonna be in the dance contest? Who's going to sing? You better sing your ass off." I wanted them to know they could be part of that world. A couple of the kids from the program who used to be gangsta do lights and sound now. One girl does background vocals for different artists. So, I guess it worked. I will admit, though, taking kids to sets was also a little selfish because I wanted to see the ins and outs of putting a show together for myself.

Eventually, the seeds I'd planted like Johnny Appleseed across Hollywood bloomed. Those people I'd hung out with on different sets or passed out comp tickets to became executives or directors or casting directors. People who hire people like me. And when they needed a funny Black actress, they remembered. "You were always so sweet, you were the only one to talk to me on that set, and you always invited me to shows. How would you like to try out for this role?"

In 2015, I got cast as Nekeisha on *The Carmichael Show*. Not long after that, I started landing bigger parts in a few movies. I moved up the call sheet spot by spot by moving constantly so I could eat, like a hummingbird flapping my wings a thousand times a minute.

That's why I don't like when people say I'm a "breakout star." Makes it sound like I was in jail. I wasn't in jail. I was in the grind. I didn't just land in a blockbuster movie out of pure luck. I worked my ass off. But I believe the reason I've had success, my secret sauce, is that I live by the rule that how you treat others is how they're going to treat you. That creates good energy. I want joy for myself, so I'm always trying to bring it to others.

I would never have gotten cast in *Girls Trip* if it hadn't been for that good energy. What happened was, I did this movie *Keanu* in 2016 with Key and Peele. They play these bougie-ass cousins who front like they're hard so they can get their kitten back from the gangsters who stole it.

We shot in New Orleans. Even though it's so sticky-icky in that city you've got to wash your ass three times a day, I love New Orleans. My favorite thing is the people . . . 'cause the people make the food, and that food is *so good*. The po' boys, the muffulettas, the red beans and rice. Amazing. All that good food must put everyone who lives there in a good mood because they were all so friendly, calling me "Love" every time I turned around. Hearing that felt good on my spirit. Even if it was the raggedy, toothless dude on Bourbon Street with throw-up on his shoes saying it, it still made me happy.

Whenever I wasn't in a scene, I would hang out with the crew members just like I always did, getting to know them. Then, after we finished shooting for the day, I'd go out with the crew to the Howling Wolf. There'd be a big band in the main room where everybody would dance for a couple hours. I'd go in a little room in the back and do a comedy show. We'd eat fried pickles and have some daiquiris and let those good times roll.

Eight or nine months after we wrapped, I got a phone call from a guy who'd worked in the sound department on *Keanu*. He said that a bunch of the *Keanu* crew were working on this new movie filming in New Orleans called *Girls Trip*.

"I've got to tell you. I read this script, and all I could think about was Tiffany Haddish. This character Dina is *you*."

I thanked him and filed that information away. A few days later, someone from set decoration on *Keanu* called me and said, "Girl, you read *Girls Trip* yet? I'm telling you, you got to be part of this movie."

Over the next couple weeks, *eight* different crew members sent me that script, and they all told me, "Please don't tell nobody I gave this to you." I thought, *Dang, if this many different people are risking their asses to tell me I need to take a look at this script, I guess I need to read it.* I did and my immediate reaction was, "Who was kicking it with me last summer and knows how I get down with my girls? This character *is* me. I got to get this part."

I called my agents.

"You hear about *Girls Trip*? Can you get me an audition for that movie?"

"Sorry, Tiffany, we know about it, but they only want to see names."

Names? They meant people who had enough name recognition to open a movie.

"Look, you tell them I've had a name since 1979, and it's Tiffany Fucking Haddish. You better get me an audition or at least a pre-read or something, 'cause I got to do this movie." So, they got me a pre-read.

I went in, and the studio had me read in front of an *intern*. Not for the casting director. Not for the assistant casting director. An intern. That was not what I had been hoping for, but okay. Fine. I'm a professional; I'll do my job. So, I read for the part, and *I fucking killed it*.

The producers called me for another read for the casting director's assistant. Killed it *again*. Then they called me to read for the casting director. *De-mol-ished* it.

Afterward, they said, "You know what? You're pretty amazing. We'll be in touch."

But I still didn't have the part. I had to go back in one last time for an audition with the director himself, Malcolm Lee, one of the few Black men who has climbed the directing ranks.

On the day of that audition, I was in the waiting room for two hours while all the big actresses were trying out for Dina. I should have been nervous, but I was just goofing around, flirting with this hot dude who was there, leaning my head on him, laughing. Even though there was a lot of talent in that lobby, I was thinking, *That role is* mine.

When my name was called, I went into the room and looked around, but I didn't see Malcolm Lee anywhere. Turns out, he was already in New Orleans setting up for the movie, so we were going to do it as a Skype audition. They set up the laptop, fixed the lighting and stuff. I could see Malcolm on the screen at his desk with a wall covered in Post-its behind him. Now this was several years before COVID, so the only time I had done video calls before was for phone sex. When I saw that video screen, I instantly went, "I'm about to take my clothes off!"

I told Malcolm, "I'm gonna tell you right now, bro. I'm gonna do this, but this is not normal for me. I'm used to being sexy for my man in this kind of situation. You got some nice lighting, and there's some Post-its on that wall behind you like you got a job, and I smell that good credit from here. If I start to unbutton my shirt or pull something down, please bring me back to reality."

He laughed. "All right. Let's get to the scene."

I did the scene and when I finished, he said, "That was very good. Can you do it less 'urban'?"

Mind you, this scene was written very "urban." But could I take all the urban out of it? Hell yeah, I could. I went to school in the Valley.

So I gave him a little "*Ohmigod, Amber, this is crazy,*" all Valley girl like. Malcolm busted up laughing. Then he asked me if I could do it *more* urban.

Again, hell yeah, I could. I did Dina to the max, and I had Malcolm cracking up. I walked out of there feeling very confident.

But then a week went by—total silence.

Finally, at long last, two days before rehearsals were scheduled to start, I got a phone call from my agent: *She ready.*

Girls Trip changed my life, and it never would have happened if I hadn't been down with the crew—if they hadn't liked me enough to think to send me that script even when they thought they might get in trouble for sneaking it to me. That whole time I'd been grinding, I'd been building my network of sleeper cells, people who were ready to back me up when it was time to move. I learned that from watching the white man.

The white man knows how to stick together with his people. You watch an Adam Sandler movie or a Judd Apatow movie or a Wes Anderson movie, it's the same faces in different costumes. They put their friends in their movies, in their shows, whatever they produce. I'm not hating on them. I get it. I like to work with the people I like to work with, too. It's fun. Who wouldn't want to work with their friends if they were given the chance to? Like it's a party every day? The trick is you just have to get that one person in through the door to hold it open for everyone else to come to the party.

Girls Trip grossed $140 million worldwide. Things started popping off for me for real after that. One of my friends said, "Tiffany, you're the gatekeeper now." She meant it as a compliment, like, *You a bad bitch*, but I was like, "Fuck that, I don't want to be a gatekeeper. I want to take the screws out of the hinges of the gate, take off the door, and lay it down so my people can just walk on through." Come on in, y'all. *Girls Trip* meant I was going to have a chance to use my pull, to move the way the white man moved, and bring my friends along with me for the journey like Dorothy in *The Wizard of Oz*.

Not everyone has been on board with this approach. Even my own team occasionally opposes people I want on my projects, telling me who I should not put on or work with. When I push back, they say, "Tiffany, you're being difficult to work with, a diva." I know that "diva" is code for "bitch." You know what I say to that? If I were a white man, you wouldn't be pushing me on this. I want you to treat me like I have a pink penis and I'm from Australia. Me and my big pink penis need to get paid, and we need to bring the other dicks up with us.

That's why I negotiated with Netflix the way I did for my second special, *Black Mitzvah*.

Back in 2018, Netflix offered me a deal for a comedy special. It was a good deal, but not *the best* deal, not like generational wealth kind of deal. Not like private jet kind of deal. If I had just started doing comedy ten years ago, the offer would have been cool, but as I've explained, I had a lot of experience under my belt. I told the executives their number wasn't going to do it for me. Netflix came back and said, "Hey, well, how about we give you this much more?" and that number was a lot more. Not Amy Schumer more or Chris

Rock more—nowhere near Jerry Seinfeld more—but substantially more. Maybe not a private jet, but certainly first class for life. That was interesting, and I certainly considered signing the contract right then and there. But these negotiations were going down right around the time my girl Mo'Nique was talking about boycotting Netflix because they were not doing enough for inclusion.

She wasn't wrong. Of the seventy or so specials Netflix had made before 2018, there were only about a dozen women showcased, and guess how many of those women were Black? Did you guess zero? You fucking should have. You're telling me there wasn't one single funny Black woman worth a half an hour on Netflix? Not one? And you gave Larry the Cable Guy a platform? For real? I could go on your average city bus and find a woman who deserved time more than some of these mediocre white dudes they'd featured.

She had me thinking she was right. Netflix needed more inclusion. I was going to see what I could do to give Netflix a nudge. I wanted to see more people who look like me working. I wanted to tell our stories. I made Netflix a proposition: "How about this—instead of giving me more money, why don't you guys allow me to produce a stand-up comedy special for some comics that I choose? I want to share the platform. The money you could have paid me, let's give it to them. Present them to the world in a separate showcase. And *then* I'll agree to do my special."

I thought they would say no. I was *sure* they would say no. But they called me up and said, "You got a deal. Pick six comics, whoever you want. You present the show. You shoot it however you want to shoot it. Go for it."

"For real?"

"For real."

"Oh, we about to have it popping!"

As I was busting my ass coming up, I wished so much that someone had just called me up and said, "Tiffany, here's your special.

Here's your chance to shine. I'm going to vouch for you." Now I could do that for other women. Be like their Fairy Godmother. Or their Uncle Mort. Wanda Sykes came on board as a producer, and I hand-picked women who had been good to me, who looked out for me, gave me words of encouragement, helped me move, drove me home from the airport, or just made me laugh super damn hard. These were some of the women I'd told, "If I ever get anywhere in life, I'm pulling you with me." I am a woman of my word. If I say I'm gonna do it, that's what I'm gonna do. They'd given me that good energy, and I wanted to give it back because real bitches look out for each other.

Every woman I had in mind had a story like mine. They knew struggle. They hadn't had anything handed to them, but they weren't bitter or sad. They were laughing their way to healing. First person I thought of was Flame Monroe because Flame makes me laugh so hard, and I love her journey. To watch her tell jokes about being a single parent and a Black trans woman who never gives up? She is just a beast onstage. I knew I had to involve her in the project. Aida Rodriguez—she'd been homeless for a spell, just like me. Marlo Williams—she grew up in the foster system, just like me. April Macie—she'd been grinding nearly as long as I had and had grown up poor as hell. Chaunté Wayans—yes, she's a Wayans, but she's also a lesbian, which isn't the easiest thing to deal with in the comedy world. And Tracey Ashley was just funny as fuck to me.

I called them up. "You ready? You better get ready 'cause you about to light it up."

Every single one of those women was so fucking excited about the opportunity 'cause they knew what it would mean not just for their careers but for the people who hadn't ever seen their experience represented in a Netflix special before. In a promotional interview, Flame talked about hoping there was some little kid in a room somewhere who would see her and know it was okay to live as who you are. Representation isn't just checking off boxes; it's validating experience.

Everyone wants to feel like their life counts. I see you out there, Anton. You do you.

The women on *They Ready* have shows of their own about to come out, cartoons, movies. That right there is more to me than money. It is food for the soul to see my friends shine, to know their children will have better opportunities.

One of my goals is to make eighty films by the time I'm fifty. Every time I make a movie, that creates jobs for fifty to two hundred people. While I'm at it, I'm using nepotism at its finest. You want me to be in your studio? You need to grab some of these foster youth from my hood. They need to intern for you. I can't work with you if you're not taking some of my kids. I want to see us working. Help create generational wealth.

When I was growing up, my grandma used to tell me, "We are all just big balls of energy. You can be positive energy or negative energy. What kind are you going to be? Are you going to be someone people want to be around or someone who makes people want to go away?" I choose positive. I choose the kind of energy that brings people together instead of pushing them apart.

Lifting other people up feels like something I have an obligation to do, like when you see somebody's car broken down in the middle of the street. You could gawk at them, be like, "Them's the breaks! Tough luck." Or you could put down your purse, roll up your sleeves, and give them a push. You give them a little shove, they get some momentum, turn that ignition, and *vroom*, they're on their way, holding on to the steering wheel. That car won't stop for a long-ass time. And everybody's happier because a system breakdown isn't keeping people from getting where they want to go.

BLESSINGS

WHAT I WANT TO know is why so many people have thought it was their job to tell me how to wear my hair over the course of my life.

Like, back when I was sixteen, I was dating this boy named Nate. He didn't go to my school, but we talked on the phone a lot and sometimes we met up over at the Crenshaw Mall. My homegirl Mona was dating his brother, so the two of us would ride over to their place during the summer to hang out and talk, maybe make out with them a little. Then Mona broke up with Nate's brother, so I would take the bus over to see Nate by myself. Our relationship was pretty chill. I was just having a good time with him.

One sticky afternoon, after we'd been kissing on each other, Nate pulled back so he could see my face and said, "You know, you would be so much more attractive if your hair was longer."

I touched my hair. I usually wore it tucked back in a little bun with Shirley Temple bangs, but that day, I'd gotten a press and curl, so it was down. "What do you mean? My hair's already past my shoulders."

"Yeah, but you'd be prettier if it was down to your butt. You should get a weave."

This was back around '96, when everyone from Aaliyah and Mariah to Janet and Toni was rocking long hair, but I didn't know what a weave was.

"You want me to get a what? You talking about a wig? I'm not spending my money on no wigs. I'm already buying bus passes so I can come see your sorry ass." Even though Nate was a casual thing, it still hurt my feelings when he said I wasn't pretty enough as I was. I already felt like shit about how I looked anyway because of my mom. She told me I was ugly all the damn time, especially after her accident when she turned mean as hell. Her speech came back after a few months, but it seemed like her mind only had space for the most hurtful words. The things she said burned so deep they set fire to my insides. I still feel the burn in my intestines.

To this day, I can hear poison in her voice when she caught me looking at myself in the mirror for too long. "Get out that mirror. Who do you think you are? We don't have vain people in this house. You don't need a mirror to see you ugly as sin."

Ouch, Mom. Why'd you have to go and say that? I stared at my reflection. *You know what? She right. My ears is too small for my head, and my nose look funny.* And then I got my ass whupped. I'd love to tell you it didn't matter how other people saw me, but when your mom tells you you're not beautiful, you believe it and it hurts like a motherfucker. Once she'd planted the idea I was ugly, it was like a cactus needling the inside of my brain—didn't take much to keep it alive.

Like most women, I've done a million things to my body to make myself feel prettier. I've put on war paint like I was getting ready to fight out there in the streets. I've put Vicks VapoRub on my skin 'cause I saw on YouTube it makes your skin brighter and gets rid of stretch marks. I think it just made my forehead minty fresh. Regina Hall told me she put tape on her face for wrinkles, so I busted out the

Scotch tape and put it all over my mug 'cause that woman *does not* look fifty. I put so much of it on I looked like a mummy while I slept. So, yeah, I've tried a lot of stuff, but I'm a basic chick. If I had my way, I'd prefer to keep my routine simple instead of going through all that before I leave the house.

But here's the thing—after the success of *Girls Trip*, my workload got heavier and so did all the appearance stuff that went with it. Basic wasn't going to cut it anymore for the red carpets and premieres and interviews where most stars spent hella cash and time getting ready. I got the lashes, the makeup, the Indian hair, the stylist, the makeup artist. It was a lot. Some days it was great because I didn't have to think about whether I looked beautiful or not. It was someone else's responsibility to make me look good, and that was one less decision I had to make.

But sometimes, when I was going through the routine, another part inside of me was like an eight-year-old shouting, "I want to wear Jordans with my church dress!" That's who I am. When I listen to the call to be myself, it sets my spirit free. But the machine tries to make you a Barbie doll. Like you being you is not right. I hated that feeling.

Eventually, I got it in my mind that I was going to shave myself bald. Not short-haired. Not peach-fuzzed. *Bald-headed.*

Every single person I mentioned my idea to tried to talk me out of it. My friends said, "Don't do it. What if your head look all messed up under there?" One friend told me I should check with my man before I cut it. Fuck that. I had had enough of men telling me how my hair should or shouldn't look. I said, "I am an adult woman. I'm not consulting with no motherfucking man about something that's growing out of *my* motherfucking body." My manager and my publicist were less direct. "Of course! Great idea. Love it . . . Oh, but you know what? You got that event coming up. Maybe now is not the best time. Maybe after this shoot wraps? Maybe in six months?" They fed me all these maybes to try to distract me and get me to forget about shaving my head, but I never forgot.

When the coronavirus lockdowns started rolling out across the world, I said to myself, "Ain't no red carpets coming up no time soon. I ain't doing a movie. And the movies I am up for want me to wear a wig. The wig's going to fit better anyway if I got no hair." I was going to shave all my hair off—I mean *all* of it—so I could see what was going on up on my head.

I really liked that idea because every religion in the world talks about the importance of knowing thyself. I already knew myself below the neck pretty good. I'd gotten myself a body chart—you know, like the ones they've got at the morgue—and I filled it out, so I knew where all my little weird dings and dents were. But I realized I didn't know what was on my head. I'd just seen bits and pieces of my skull, like this little patch I rub on the side of my head when I stress out—when I say, "This is really some shit"—to the point where I almost made a bald spot. But that was just a patch. I didn't know much about the rest of my head. What was going on with my scalp? What did it look like? Was it flat, round, smooth, wrinkly, or what? Did I have any moles up there?

I knew I had a bunch of moles on the rest of my body—101 marked on my body chart—but what about on top of my head? A dermatologist had told me I should have them checked every six months, but in forty years I hadn't checked even once if I had any on my head.

When I was little, my grandma told me, "Tiffany, everywhere you got a mole is where God kissed you. Those are your blessings." When she said that, I immediately thought about my auntie 'cause she got moles all over her—all over her neck, all on her chest, little things on her arms, everywhere. She looked like she rolled around in a box of Raisinets. I thought, "Dang, God must have really been loving on my auntie."

I used to have two moles on my face. Now I just have one 'cause I had one removed from my chin. When I was around twenty, something funky happened with the mole I had there and my chin swelled up like Will Smith's face in *Hitch*. I went to the doctor, and they said, "Oh, there's *definitely* something going on in there. We're going to have to remove that."

I got to the appointment for my first plastic surgery—my *only* plastic surgery—at Kaiser Permanente. They were going to put me to sleep. I said, "Oh, hell no. If you got to put me to sleep, I'm not going to do this." So they gave me the same stuff the dentist gives you; they numbed my whole jaw and got to work. I could hear the sawing, the cutting, the buzzing like they had a chain saw in that office, but I didn't feel a thing. And then the doctor started pulling at the mole, tugging at it, tugging at it, tugging at it. Finally, he yanked on it real hard and stretched what he'd dug out in front of me—long wiry strands. It looked like there were telephone cables coming out of my face.

The doctor said, "No wonder it was so swollen. You have all these ingrown hairs." He showed me this clump of hair twitching like a spider on the forceps. When he dropped the tangle of black hairs in the tray, I was surprised the damn thing didn't run away.

"Well, we might as well go ahead and take off the one under your eye, too."

"Nahooooo. Daaey woooonn reh niiiiiize meeee. Daaey woooonn reh niiiiiize meeee." I couldn't get the words out right 'cause the whole lower half of my face was malfunctioning.

I was used to that mole under my eye. It wasn't my favorite feature, but I took some comfort in seeing it every morning when I looked in the mirror. *Yep, that's me, the one with the mole under my eye.* I was afraid nobody would recognize me without it. That's what I was trying to say to the doctor, "They won't recognize me." I didn't necessarily love that mole, but it was part of me, part of who I am, and I wasn't about to let that man take that from me. So, I still have that one mole under my eye.

Anyway, I wanted to find out how many more blessings I had. I'd been talking about shaving my head for a minute. I was done talking about it. I was gonna *be* about it.

One afternoon during lockdown, I invited a few of my friends over and set up the camera on my phone for the whole world to watch on Instagram Live as I cut off all my hair. At the time, I had locs that just grazed my shoulders. They were in decent shape, but I was ready to get rid of them, to feel lighter.

I hit "record" and announced, "I'm cutting this hair off!" I piled my locs up on top of my head so I could get to the part underneath where I got that 4C hair. My hair is about unity. Every single strand wants to be entwined with other strands; they're so united I have broken those "unbreakable" combs before. I raised the scissors and my one friend yelled at me not to do it, but I said, "I do what I want to do!" As I grabbed one loose loc, she said, "Ohmigod, Tiff, wait." But too late. I did it. My friends were losing their minds, talking about how they needed a full stomach to watch what I was doing, but I was loving it. They started arguing about which restaurant had the best breakfast food. My girl was hating on Waffle House, which is some bullshit because Waffle House is the bomb, and besides, I've seen her eat like 85 percent of my breakfast when we go there.

One loc after another hit the floor and my silhouette transformed. It was ashy as hell up there because I had had those locs in a long time. There was a minute halfway through where things looked a little wild with a chunk of my scalp showing. My friends were freaking out, screaming at me that I was making a mistake. But it was just hair. I wasn't the first woman to cut her hair off. A good stylist can work with anything. Girls get in the chair with no hair and they come out looking like mermaids. I kept going, and with every cut, I felt freer. Like I was hacking away at all the bullshit. *Snip. Goodbye, braids so tight they give me a headache. Snip. Goodbye, spending forty-five minutes to an hour trying to figure out my style. Snip. Goodbye, sore arms from holding them over my head, twisting, combing, pinning.* By the end, I was back to the original edition of what God made. *Hello, Basic Model Tiff. Hello, me.*

I saved some of the hair I'd cut off for my Bible. You put your hair in the Bible, it comes back stronger. That's why they put a baby's hair in there, 'cause then it's protected by the Word.

When I was done, I had sort of a halo all around my head. I looked like I was from the '80s. I also kinda looked like my uncle Charles—he was born in 1930—only somehow, I looked *good.* Men would still fuck. And, oh my god, it felt so good to comb it and run my fingers through it; it was soft and a little bouncy.

At that point, I still had like a half inch of hair, and I wanted to go all the way so the rest of my head would match my forehead, but I needed to wait a couple days for the wrinkles to ease out of my skull. Later that night, I rubbed some berries and juices from my garden on my head, then put some kale smoothie on there to let my scalp settle and smooth out.

A few days later, I was in Mississippi. It was a cloudy day, the air wet and heavy, but I felt easy breezy as I sat down to shave off the last half inch of hair. Swipe. Swipe. Swipe—but careful so blood didn't get all over. Before long, I was squeaky clean. My mama must have pushed me out of her birth canal just right because I have a nice-shaped head.

My fingertips got to know my bald-ass scalp. *Hi there, scalp. It's nice to meet you. Let's see what you're about. You know what? You sorta smooth like a penis. That's pretty nice. You're a little flat in the back, but that's okay. All right, what else you got? Okay, here's two more moles. That makes 103. I guess God love me a lot, too. Hold up, what is this part that feels like I got a chewed-up meat head?* I twisted my mirror around and saw two scars I had forgotten I had.

I touched way in the back and right away I remembered where that chewed-up part was from. When I was in first grade, I'd been out on the playground ruling the tetherball court. I was bouncing around on my toes, grunting, "ARGGH!" like I was Serena Williams. I must have hit the tetherball way too hard because when it came back around, it went *BAM!* Right in my face. My head hit the ground like someone had coldcocked me. Busted the back of my head wide open. Next thing I knew, the school nurse was giving me ice packs and trying to stop the bleeding using compression. It was a big cut, so there was a ton of blood. Turns out you've got a lot of blood vessels in your scalp.

Me and my sisters and brothers were still living with my mom at the time, so the nurse called her up to the school to come get me. My mom arrived, took a look at my head bleeding all over the nurse's office, and she went, "It ain't that bad. Let's go." I think the nurse was surprised at my mom's reaction because, like I said, there was *a lot* of blood.

My mom didn't have the resources for certain things. And I guess we didn't have insurance. It wasn't like we were starving, but money was tight. Or I don't know. Maybe we did have insurance, and she just didn't feel like dragging me to the doctor because she was beat. She was a manager at the post office, worked the graveyard shift, and didn't get home until five o'clock in the morning. She also had her own business, plus us kids to take care of. My bloody head was just more bullshit to add to her to-do list.

She took me home, cut off the hair around the wound, and stuffed some toilet paper into the cut like you do in your underwear when you get your period and you don't have a pad. Then she covered it with a Band-Aid and a little bit of tape and pulled my hair back to close the gash. She pulled so hard it was like she was trying to pull the thoughts out my head. I looked real funny because she'd put one ponytail on top, then pulled a second ponytail around the back. I looked like a chickenheaded Snork.

That was why I had a meat head on the back of my skull—because I'd got a hair tie instead of stitches.

Then there was the other scar I found when I was feeling around on my new penis head.

You know how when you do some stupid shit people ask you, "What's the matter with you? Were you dropped on your head as a child?" Yeah, well, I was. When I was six, my mama was helping me get out of the car, and I don't know what happened exactly, but somehow I slipped through her arms. She was just like "Whoops" and accidentally dropped me. My head hit the sidewalk. Hard. Bring on the blood.

That time I'd gotten stitches. She put me right back in the car and took me to the hospital, but on the way there she told me I was not allowed to tell the doctor how my head got broke. She said, "You just say you fell out the car." Now that I'm older, I'm guessing my mom was probably paranoid because a year or so earlier we had had a car accident while me and my cousins were in the back seat, no seat belts. On impact, we all flew forward, and my cousins fell on top of me. My left leg just snapped. Even though I was pretty little, I remembered all the questioning in the ER that day about what exactly happened that resulted in my broken leg. Where had we been sitting? How many of us were in the car? Who was driving? What intersection? Just endless questions. Like maybe there was something my mom wasn't telling them. Like maybe they didn't believe it was a car accident that broke my leg.

So, when she dropped me on my head, my mom knew the doctors were going to look at my medical record and see I had just been there with a broken leg and now here I was with a big fat bloody cut on my head. Now, maybe a white family comes in with a kid who has been in the ER twice in two years and the staff goes, "Oh, how unfortunate. Two accidents? You poor thing. What are the chances? Don't worry. We'll take care of everything." But when you're Black and you roll through the doors with a kid bleeding from her head and a sketchy story, an investigation is launched and Child Protective Services gets involved. We needed none of that and my mom knew it, so she asked me to say I fell.

When you're young, you do whatever your mama wants. That's the queen. You go, *This person feeds me, puts clothes on my back, puts a roof over my head; I'm gonna worship her.* You don't know who God is when you're born, so your mom is God until you learn otherwise. That's how I felt about my mother. My whole world revolved around her.

I used to make these mud pies for my mom to show her how much I loved her. I'd go out in the yard and grab heavy handfuls of mud, then I would stomp back into the house, take all the spices and seasonings I could get out of our cabinet, mix everything together, and form it into a patty. I'd tiptoe into my mom's room and push a plate of mud and cinnamon under her nose. "These are for you, Mommy, because you work so hard. You're the best working mommy ever." She'd lift half an eyelid and say, "Thank you very much. Now let working mommy sleep." I'd go clean up the kitchen while I waited for her to get out of bed. When she emerged, she'd pick me up and give me the best hug—the kind where you feel like you're fully inside that person's body. She'd bring me into herself so deep that you couldn't even see me from behind. I could take a deep breath and let out any pain I was feeling into her. I still dream about those hugs.

She wasn't perfect, but I loved her. If she wanted me to say I fell out the car, okay, I was going to say that. When the doctor came in, I straight-up told him, "I fell out of the car."

I didn't really lie. I *did* fall out the car. I might have had help by being dropped a little bit, but I still fell.

I just wanted to please my mama, to do the right thing and get her approval. We all want to feel that our god approves of us.

You might not be able to see all of them, but I've got a lot of scars. My life has been far from perfect. Like I said, my dad walked out on me when I was three. I watched my mama turn mad unpredictable after her car accident. I lived in foster homes. I've been put in the county building, pulled out the goddamn county building, put on the street, stayed in homeless shelters, slept in my car, been disrespected, been violated, been hurt. I have had to fight for every damn thing I have, and I have the battle scars to prove it.

But you know what? Scar tissue is strong as hell. When a horse gets a cut, the skin that grows back into a hard scar is called proud flesh. That sounds about right to me. I'm proud of how what I've been through has made me grow back stronger.

Going through shit has also made me more compassionate. When I encounter someone who is rude or nasty, I don't always assume they were born a dick. I have empathy for them because obviously some- thing happened where they feel like they need to be nasty. Their spirit is messed up. So, I pray for them.

Some people have had no struggle, experienced no injustice. They don't even know what that feels like. They might see it on TV, but that's not their life. They're like, "Everything seems fair to me. I got my education paid for. As soon as I graduated, I got to work at my dad's firm. I got land. What's the problem?" They haven't had to fight for anything. But I haven't met one single, successful person who hasn't had some kind of struggle—something they had to handle before they made it to the next level.

All the weight I carried in my life has made me strong as fuck. Your experiences mold you, make you who you are. If things had panned out differently, if I had been raised by rich parents in the suburbs, maybe I would be a spoiled brat with an inheritance. Maybe I'd have a nine-to-five customer service job. I might not be funny at all if I had not gone through everything I have gone through. I would just be a pretty face with undiscovered talent. Everything that hurt me, that made me feel bad, I used it. Everything that I am capable of, everything I am able to access in my comedy, it grew after tragedy. 'Cause you know what shit is? Shit is fertilizer; it makes you grow.

Pain is like a gift. A gift I don't want all the time, mind you, but once I have it, I figure out a way to make it a blessing. Some of your blessings are going to be heavy.

There are days when I imagine another world where my mom never had that car accident—a world where she stayed home sick from work that day and she never had her head go through that windshield and I ended up with a mom who put Lunchables in my lunch box and fought with me about my curfew when I was a teenager. When she has calm, quiet moments, I see that woman inside her, but I can't reach her.

In my selfish ideal world, I meet somebody magical who can heal people like out of *The Green Mile*. Michael Clarke Duncan takes my mom into his huge-ass hands, blows on her gently until a halo of light glows, and all the bad floats out the window away from her. She's got all her cognition back, and I have the mom I remember.

But I know that's just a movie. Here in the real actual world, I have to understand my mother has a mental illness. It is hard to look at someone you love and see their brain is not well. I don't know if those genes were in her and they would have kicked in at some point no matter what or if the accident smashed her up so bad that it broke open whatever was containing the illness that spilled all over her brain. Either way, a lot was out of her control as I was growing up, which meant there were dozens of mom things she could not do—not because she didn't want to but because she wasn't operating with all the tools necessary to raise five kids. Maybe the cockeyed way my mom loved me was the way I was supposed to be loved, and that's why I am the way I am today. Maybe that's why my heart is a sensitive instrument that responds like it does. Maybe that's why I'm cursed with joy and the need to share it with everyone.

✦

Recently, my mom was taking care of my animals while I was out of town. She hadn't taken care of anything by herself like that since we were kids, but I needed someone to feed my cat and my dogs and get them some exercise while I was shooting *Haunted Mansion*. A few days into my trip, my sister called. "Tiff, you are not going to believe this. Mom's doing *so good*. She's not talking to herself. Not getting all mad. She's talking to your pets. She's loving them, walking them, cleaning them. I've never seen her smile so much in my life."

What do you know? Now, I had no intention of giving my mom my animals—I needed my animals back—but when I got back from filming, I got her a beautiful dog: a bulldog we called Satin. I tell you, my mom was lit up. I haven't seen her shine like that since I was seven. She was so happy. She was hugging the dog, hugging me. She's been sleeping with it, washing it, buying it outfits.

Seeing her with Satin, I realized she needed something to take care of. She was at her best when she was taking care of us kids, even if the way she was doing it wasn't perfect. Fixing up my busted head, getting me the care I needed at the hospital even though she didn't know what they were going to think about her—those were some of her best moments.

With my head as bald as a baby's bottom, I could really see myself. My hair had been like a frame, and a frame can distract from what's in it. Shaving my head was like taking a painting out of a really big frame and putting it on a white wall so I could see it for real.

You know how babies act when they first discover themselves in the mirror? I felt like that. *Look at this! Ohmigosh. You're beautiful. Look at you. All of you. Every part. You look pretty, girl. Look at those eyes.*

Those eyes are actually really good. They spaced out nice. Look at that nose. It's cute. Look at those lips God made. God did such a good job with you. Kudos to you, God.

I looked into the pupils of my eyes and fell in love with myself. I felt like I really knew me now, head to toe. Nobody could tell me about me like I can tell me about me. Not my mama, not publicists, not sixteen-year-old Nate.

I touched the scars on my bald head. I wasn't mad at my mom for taping up my skull instead of getting me stitches or for asking me to lie in that hospital. She was a Black woman with a bleeding baby who was scared she was going to have that baby taken away. We all have our pain.

I went outside where it had started to rain. The wind blew, and I got goose bumps on my scalp. The raindrops felt like God was giving me a million little kisses all over my head. Like I was being blessed or baptized by these amazing sensations. I started to cry a little bit. Forty years on this planet, and I had never felt anything like that before.

If I died and went to heaven or purgatory and they told me, "Man, you here already? That's too bad 'cause you missed out on *this* sensation," and then they gave me a little taste of that feeling of the rain on my head, of loving myself, of knowing myself all over, scars and all? I'd be furious. I'd be like, "Send me back. How do I get back there? Where's the return ticket booth?" But I didn't miss it. I was there for it as I stood outside with the rain showering my bald-ass head, covering me and all my blessings.

HONEYPOT

THERE ARE A LOT of bees in my yard right now. I'm not complaining. I got them on my property on purpose. A company called Flamingo Estates put together a fundraiser where they set up hives on different celebrities' properties so they can sell the honey. When they pitched the idea to me, they said if I was going to participate, I had to keep the bees for six months. The money they made would support an organization that helped kids stay in school and provided them with housing. I know what it's like not to have housing as a kid, so I said "sign me up."

A beekeeper brought over a Tiffany blue wooden box that said "Flamingo" on the outside. When I saw that, I thought, *I'm about to get some flamingos!* But then I remembered about the bees. The box is kind of like a filing cabinet, with drawers to hold the honeycomb. He set it up next to my angel's trumpet tree that has these big, beautiful blossoms that dangle with their mouths open to the earth.

After the beekeeper left, the bees started coming out and checking out the garden. I didn't want to get too close—I wasn't trying to get stung—so I stayed on the porch and watched them explore. I let them be and they let me be.

The beekeeper came by every couple weeks to check in on my bees as they buzzed around. I got used to having them out there, and as I got used to them, I started getting closer and closer. I'd lean on their box watching them come and go, and they paid me no mind. Every once in a while, one would sit on my shoulder. I talked to them, telling them about my day, making jokes. I combined my plant-based comedy with bee comedy. The bees are a better audience, 'cause at least they make noise, unlike my rude-ass plants.

I'm excited about having bees 'cause I know they help your garden grow. I love my garden. If you grow your own food, you'll always be able to eat no matter what's going on in your career. You get fired from a gig, you can come home and make yourself a kale smoothie and you're all good. My family has had gardens as far back as I can remember. My grandmother's people were share-croppers and she kept up that tradition, minus the backbreaking labor and exploitation. I spent a lot of time in the fruit trees she had growing all around the house—pomegranate trees, lemon trees, orange trees. There was a eucalyptus tree, a nectarine tree, a peach tree, a walnut tree. (Let me tell you something, do not plant walnut trees just anywhere because rats will show up. Rats and squirrels will be fucking up your walnuts.) I'd eat avocados and plums from the trees during the day, then be on the toilet all night. I had the best moving bowels in all of South Central. My stomach was very flat.

Now that I've got my own garden, I'm in it all the time. Sometimes, I go out there in my evening gown after an event. It'll be dark outside, and I'll turn on my flashlight and check on my plants like a sexy burglar. It feels good to take care of things. There's something about raising a plant up from a little seed, making sure it gets what it needs, that fills up my soul.

As soon as spring came round, my bees started swarming. I came out of the house one day and they had covered the entire trumpet tree—and my little marijuana plant I have growing out there (no snitching)—with their bee bodies piled on top of one another, humming this off-key song. I tiptoed over to see what was going on, and they started coming off the tree in droves. They circled the backyard like a big dark cloud. If it had been a cartoon, they would have formed an arrow and come for me, but instead they lifted up into the sky past the power cables and split off—some to the east, some to the west. I walked over to the hive and opened up the drawers. There were just a few bees hanging out. Had all my bees just left me? Had I been dumped by my bees? I was starting to feel rejected, but within like forty-five minutes, they came back.

The next time I saw the beekeeper, he explained my bees were doing what they'd been put on this planet to do, putting in work. They were teaching the newer bees how to fly, teaching them how to collect pollen, and, probably, some of them were also getting it on with their queen.

Apparently, when it's time for honey bees to mate they go out on the town. They don't shit where they eat. They do it in midair like some aerial sex acrobatics. The male drones die as soon as they do their thing, but the queen survives. She can produce up to two thousand eggs each day. That is one busy female. She spends her whole dang life having bee babies.

Growing up, I thought that was going to be me. I'd have a bunch of kids—maybe not two thousand, but maybe five kids by four baby daddies. I'd collect that county check. Nearly everybody in my neighborhood had kids. If I had a boy, I was going to call him Illuminate because he would light up a room. Nate for short. If I had a girl, she'd be named Clarity. I imagined myself standing in the doorway, calling, "Clarity, I need you right now!" Life hasn't worked out that way for me, for good and bad. Mostly for good.

I have been pregnant a few times, but none of them went to term. It's not like I was looking to have a baby by any of those men, but I believe in following God's path for me. If one of those pregnancies would have ended with a baby, I would have brought it as a mom. So far, though, God's path for me seems to be for me to remain child-free because my body is not about holding onto babies. I've lost more than my fair share of pregnancies over the years. The most recent one was just a few months ago, actually.

In the past, when I've miscarried, I've kept it to myself. That's my private business. I do not want to talk about it. What is anybody gonna be able to do? They're not God. They can't undo what is going on inside me. For some reason, though, this time, I told my friend and music manager about it because he called right after it happened. He wanted me to go out, which I most definitely did not want to do. I tried to play it cool.

"Nah, I'm good. I'ma stay in tonight," I told him.

"Come on, get up, girl. We gonna go to the club."

"I don't want to go nowhere."

I wanted to just curl up in a little corner by myself, but my dude would not let up. "Tiffany, stop being like that. Let's dance."

I finally said, "I don't feel like dancing. I just lost a baby."

That shut him up about dancing. He is a good guy, so he immediately offered to pull up and take care of me. I said no, I was good and didn't need any help, because my body bending over and bleeding was normal to me. I was used to dealing with a lot of pain in my uterus. I wanted to do what I have always done in that situation, which was to load up on the ibuprofen, sleep every chance I got, lick my wounds, wonder what the fuck was wrong with my body, and then get back to pushing. I have worked through that pain many times. I almost never took time off my schedule to deal with it. I've been on set, a big bulky pad between my legs, telling myself I needed to quit thinking about why my uterus was broken and get back to work. In fact, when my friend called, I was working. I was in the middle of an interview with a reporter.

I've had a horrible time with my cycle since I was thirteen. Starting with my fourth or fifth time having my period, my body puckered up in agony each time I bled. Every month, it was the most excruciating pain you can imagine. I wanted to topple over 'cause I was so shredded up. It took it out of me. I fell asleep in class all the time, and, ohmigod, I was so damn irritable. I would get in full-blown Rumble in the Jungle fights with my siblings or anyone else who looked at me sideways. When I complained about how uncomfortable I was at school, they sent me to the nurse's office where she'd hand me a Tylenol, which my pain looked at and went, "That's cute."

I couldn't understand why no one else seemed to be feeling what I was feeling. None of my friends in high school showed any signs that their insides were on fire for a quarter of their lives. Were they just really good at pretending? How could this possibly be normal? Maybe it was all in my head. Maybe I was making a big deal out of nothing and I just needed to suck it up.

Sometimes, the pain would be so bad, I'd get in the car and just scream at the top of my lungs. I hurt so much, especially once I started having sex. Anytime I was dealing with a whole lot of meat, it would feel like I was being harpooned, like someone was stabbing me in the throat. I'd mark time, wondering how much longer I was going to have my insides torn up. I'd take it as long as I could and then I'd push my man away and say, "How about I go make you a sandwich?" I made a lot of sandwiches.

That created problems in my relationships. I guess you can only push someone away so many times before they stay away. But I thought that's just the way it was for every woman.

A man I dated used to say that his grandma told him if a woman complained about her period, it meant she was weak. I hate feeling weak, so I stopped complaining.

I told my friend all of this and he got real insistent that what I was describing wasn't normal. He gave me the number for a specialist he knew about. He's gay as hell, so I don't know how he knew a coochie doc, but he did. He promised that this doctor ran in some big-time circles. She wasn't just a doctor to the stars, she was a doctor to queens and princesses. She'd get to the bottom of it, he said. And you know what? She did.

It's not like I hadn't ever gone to doctors before. It was torture to get a speculum up in me, but I got examined a bunch of times to try to figure out what was going on with me. During one of those exams when I was in my thirties, I learned about my small, heart-shaped uterus. The doctor told me even though I had a lot of eggs, it'd be highly unlikely for me to be able to carry a baby. They offered to perform surgery to straighten it right out and improve the chances I have some kids. But I said, "I don't know. Maybe this God's birth control." By that point in my life, I felt like having kids wasn't for me. I wasn't built for it.

There's actually a small possibility I might have had some kids out there somewhere. I donated a bunch of eggs back in my twenties when I needed the money. I had to inject myself in the belly every day and drive myself all the way out to Orange County for exams. I was not allowed to have sex with anybody while I was on their program because I'd be dropping anywhere from five to twenty-five eggs, which meant if a sperm even looked at me, I'd have a whole litter of babies. The clinic was supposed to send me a check if somebody picked my eggs.

I never got that wrecked about not being a mom. People tell me I gotta try it once, but I feel like that's not my purpose. I think kids are beautiful. They're a wonderful gift from God. You love 'em, you're looking at the mini version of yourself growing up, you're happy they're here on this planet. That's amazing. And yet, I've seen so much pain and suffering, I don't know about bringing another soul into this mess.

I know that there are people out there who feel like you aren't a full woman if you don't have kids, but that's bullshit. There are so many other ways to spread your love and joy in the world. We've all got different roles to play. Different gifts to give.

Look at my bees. They've all got different jobs they're doing. You got a lot of ways to live your best bee life if you're a bee. There's the queen, of course, but then you've got your workers who do everything from producing food for the babies, making honey, building honeycomb, foraging for nectar, guarding the hive, scouting places to make a hive, and, of course, dancing. They give us honey for our tea and wax for candles and ingredients for soaps and makeup. The internet says Madam Tussauds even uses beeswax to make their mannequins. Nobody's gonna tell those bees they aren't living fully just 'cause they aren't churning out babies.

When the six months of the fundraiser was over, Flamingo Estates called and told me they were going to come pick up the bees. I was not about to let anyone take my bees. I had grown to love them and they have grown to love me. We're in a relationship. I told Flamingo Estates I would buy the bees, and now they're thriving in the hood, bringing life to the garden and honey to the table. My angel's trumpet tree is only supposed to bloom once or twice a year, but it is constantly blooming now because of the work my bees are putting in. They make eight jars of honey every two weeks because my bees have that Haddish hustle.

I decided to go to the doctor my friend recommended. It was not cheap—and they do not take insurance—but it was worth it. It was healthcare the way healthcare should be. It's messed up that the only reason I got that good treatment is because I finally have the money to afford it. She sat down and really talked to me, and more important, she listened. I told her about how every month it feels like there's people inside my uterus, scratching at the walls, trying to yank my fallopian tube inside out. How it feels like they're in there with nails like a cat's, puncturing holes all down my damn vaginal canal. How it sometimes even hurts my booty. I told her about my miscarriages. I told her about how it hurt to have sex. I told her how I was so tired. I told her everything.

She did an exam and confirmed that I did not have a heart-shaped uterus. She put an ultrasound image up on an eighty-five-inch television. I had never seen my coochie so big before. She showed me where my uterus was producing extra layers both inside and outside. Then she told me that meant I have a condition called endometriosis.

Endometriosis is when your body grows tissue that's like what's in your uterus all over your midsection. It hurts like a bitch, makes your monthly cycle really heavy, and can cause infertility. I can't believe it took until I was forty-four to learn that your cycle isn't supposed to hurt. She talked to me about different ways I could exercise and eat to help with the symptoms. The real thing she did for me, though, was let me know I wasn't crazy and I wasn't weak.

My favorite thing now is to throw endometriosis into a conversation when I'm talking with men. I'll say, "My endometriosis is kicking my ass." And they will go, "Endometrioma what? I've never heard of that. What does that do?"

I'll tell 'em, "Google it. Look it up right now and read it out." They will start reading and their eyes bug out of their face. Then they'll throw their phone on the floor like it's infectious and they want nothing to do with it. I wish that men got endometriosis. If it was painful when they ejaculated, you know they would find a cure immediately. And every doctor would know what to do to make it less painful, even a foot doctor.

During my exam, that doctor told me that I still had a lot of eggs left. Hearing that didn't make me want to have a baby or anything, but it did make me wonder about what ever did happen to those eggs I donated twenty years ago. When I got home, I dug out the receipt from my egg donation from where it was tucked into the pages of an old diary. (I'm a hoarder.) The phone number was faded, but I could still see the address for the clinic out in Orange County. I kind of remembered where it was. I drove all the way out there one sunny afternoon a week or so later. The building was the same, maybe a little darker. But as I got closer, I saw the clinic had closed up shop and it was a mental health facility now. I don't know what they did with my eggs. Maybe there's a crew of half Tiffanys out there. Or maybe the eggs are rotting next to some banana peels in a dumpster somewhere.

I'm not aiming to have a baby, but lately, I've had some restless nights where I've been out there making some poor decisions. If I got pregnant today, I'd accept whatever God's planning. But not having kids can be a blessing, too, because it gives me more time where I can be available to others. If I had my own kids, then I'd be super-focused on that and I probably wouldn't be available to do all the other things that maybe God needs me to do—like make comedy. It's really great when I get to do what I love and share it. When I hear a room giggle 'cause of a joke I told, it makes me forget about the pain going on in my body.

Who knows. Maybe someday I'll adopt. I'll get a couple of kids at like seven years old when they know how to use the bathroom already on their own. I'd want each of those kids to know, "Hey, I chose you to be here with me," and then I'd help them find their own role in the world, their own way to produce joy.

For now, I'm taking care of these bees and I'm taking care of me. I wake up at six every day. I sit outside and talk to my bees while they make their gift to the world. I'm doing good things for my body—some hula hooping moves and some stretching to get the blood flowing, a teaspoon of honey in some dandelion tea to soothe me—and I'm not hurting as much.

I've been trying to find the good in all the pain I went through each month for all those years. Maybe the pain made me stronger.

Suffering made me appreciate the good moments more. What I haven't done makes me appreciate all that I have done. And all that I've gone through has given me the strength to prepare for all I have yet to do. The future looks bright for me. I've got another special in the works, I've been writing music, buying properties, helping foster youth, and working on the grocery store. When I think about my life, the hairs on my arm get prickly, 'cause I feel so good. My honeypot might be empty, but my soul is full.

I CURSE YOU WITH JOY

THANK YOU FOR COMING on this journey with me, for listening to my stories, even if all of them weren't just hahahas. I just have one last thing to share with you before you go.

I have been put on this earth to spread joy the way fuckboys spread herpes. At the end of every show I do, I curse the audience with all the joy and happiness they can handle. So, reader, I curse you with joy, too. I curse you with joy—not strife—because if you're my enemy, adversity's just going to make you stronger. If you're my friend, you're already strong, and I want you to be happy. I hope you become so infected with love and success that, when you sneeze, you sneeze joy. When you shit, you shit success. I hope every one of you is super-happy and super-rich. I hope that your cycles come on time. If you don't want it to come, I hope it don't come. I hope the hottest motherfucker in the club asks for your number. I hope you got an office job with free food in the break room. I hope you get to jump into a clear ocean off a yacht. I hope you got a place to live, people who love you, and a community that makes you feel like you belong. I hope you are safe. I hope you know your value. And I hope you live your life as you want to, no matter what the fuck anyone else says.

I curse you with joy! Now get your ass out there and spread that shit.